FIVE BAY LANDSCAPES

UNIVERSITY OF PITTSBURGH PRESS   KAREN LUTSKY AND SEAN BURKHOLDER

Published by the University of Pittsburgh Press, Pittsburgh, Pa., 15260

Copyright © 2022, University of Pittsburgh Press

All rights reserved

Manufactured in the United States of America

Printed on acid-free paper

10 9 8 7 6 5 4 3 2 1

Cataloging-in-Publication data is available from the Library of Congress

ISBN 13: 978-0-8229-4739-4

ISBN 10: 0-8229-4739-0

Cover art: Karen Lutsky + Sean Burkholder

Cover design: Alex Wolfe

We dedicate this book to our families.

CONTENTS

viii

ACKNOWLEDGMENTS

S ALL WHO KNOW US CAN ATTEST, THIS BOOK HAS BEEN a long time coming. The two of us have been exploring the landscapes of the Great Lakes Basin academically for over a decade and personally for much longer. The investigations and inquiries of this book are not only about this place, but equally about design, action, representation, and our approach to the way we live and want to live in this world. Such work is never done alone and continues to be enriched directly and indirectly by our many colleagues, students, family members, friends, and fellow lovers of the Great Lakes Basin and design.

We begin our thanks with extending immense gratitude to our contributors and interviewees whose words are also found among these pages. We are humbled and delighted to have the opportunity to share with readers the knowledge and writings of Kyle Powys Whyte, Mae Davenport, Marcia Bjornerud, Mark Davis, and Peter Annin.

Places Journal and its editors, Nancy Levinson and Josh Wallaert, published our first collaborative texts, "Emergent Shorelines of the Great Lakes" and later "Curious Methods." We are grateful to both of them and the journal, not only for the way those pieces helped us explore the topics that are expanded upon in this book, but how that work first introduced us to Josh, who has continued to work as our editor throughout the entire writing process. Over the years he provided us with vital editorial assistance, patience, and support without which this book would likely not exist. We are also, of course, incredibly thankful to our editor Abby Collier and others at the University of Pittsburgh Press for their hard work and assistance in publishing the book.

Throughout this process we have been financially and academically supported by the institutions where we have taught, including the State University of New York at Buffalo, The Ohio State University, Pennsylvania State University, and more recently the University of

Minnesota and the University of Pennsylvania. These departments supported us with numerous grants, time, and more importantly some truly fantastic students and colleagues, many of whom have shared our love and interest in these landscapes and methods. This financial, intellectual, and emotional support has been invaluable. We offer our deepest thanks to our colleagues and friends in the field, Ron Henderson, Ozayr Saloojee, Jamie Vanucchi, Brian Davis, Rob Holmes, Joyce Hwang, Nick Rajkovich, Karen M'Closkey, Keith VanDerSys, Kristine Miller, Joe Favour, and Lynda Schneekloth who have all in their own ways inspired and advised us, shared their knowledge, and generously helped us to critically and academically advance the work and research of this book. We also want to thank the numerous research assistants who have contributed to explorations and discussions that have been formative to this text; specifically, Steven Buchanan at the University at Buffalo and Alex Marchinski at Penn State University. Likewise, we have incredible gratitude for our students who have explored both landscapes of the Great Lakes and "Curious Methods" with us over the years. Teaching brings us so much joy and their enthusiasm and curiosity have kept us afloat and our brains continuously churning surrounding us with "lovely descriptions."

Finally, we are deeply indebted to our remarkable families: Berel, Barb, Marta, and Abigail Lutsky; Mark, Bea, and Derik Burkholder; Bess Schwartz and Mary Cowan; and our many friends who have continuously supported us throughout these years. From clipping local news articles and touring coal piles with us, to hosting us and contributing to endless conversations about this work, we have been lovingly supported. Over the years, countless others have also shared their own stories, knowledge, and love of these waters and landscape with us. We will be forever honored by the generosity of time and spirit we have encountered through this process and hope we do it justice with this work.

FIVE BAY LANDSCAPES

INTRODUCTION

GREAT LAKES PERSPECTIVES

Questioning is not easy. It requires more than a critical
stance, more than simply seeing things differently; it requires
another ground altogether, one that offers different things.

—Dilip da Cunha, *The Invention of Rivers*

The shore is the interface between the earth and the water. It
is a dynamic place, a place of movement and interaction and
change.

—William Ashworth, *The Late Great Lakes*

THE WATER IS ALWAYS COLD, AND STILL IT ELICITS SURPRISE.
Feet submerged, the body acclimates to the conditions of the
moment. Toes go numb; fingers form around a stone collected
from the beach; eyes take in the horizon. At times, the shore feels
this easy—this familiar. The scale of the water and the dimensions of
change can be comprehended as directly as the stone in hand, released
to skip across a surface. But soon enough, the perspective tilts. At the
regional scale, human senses are overwhelmed by the vast reach of the
Great Lakes, the depths out of sight, the fluctuations of land, water,
climate, and species, occurring at timescales so fast and so slow that in
some ways, the landscape feels wholly unknowable.

Topographically, the Great Lakes Basin is a series of pitched surfaces, formed by glaciers, that gather water in a collection of lakes and move

◄ FIGURE 1.1. Great Lakes Shores. Shoreline views from above, along the vast and
varied littoral zone of the Great Lakes. Image by the authors.

it around slowly. Throughout this more than 200,000 square-mile region, water in various states—vapor, solid, liquid—supports and connects a rich diversity of life-forms. Much of this work happens in the littoral zone, where the water meets the land, intricately woven with social, economic, cultural, and environmental complexities and ambiguities.

People have lived with these waters for thousands of years, but since Western colonization the littoral zones have been pushed and pulled by larger anthropocentric regimes: absorbed into cells, heated and cooled, ingested, captured, deposited, scribed, washed, directed, and redirected. These moves of landscape control support population growth, landownership, and management, which, put incredible stress and expectation on the shorelines' performance and predictability, simultaneously making the "unknown" more risky and the "unpredictable" more erratic (read: climate change). Most land management is seemingly well intentioned, and some has resulted in genuine improvements. And yet water quality, habitat, and species diversity are continually threatened; equitable public access to the shore is minimal; and erosion exacerbated by hardened edges threatens homes and other infrastructure. Inevitably, the question looms: "What can, or should, people do?"

Many are interested in this question, and approaches to answering it are varied. Historians, journalists, scientists, and the like have researched these shorelines through their own methodologies and perspectives, generating insights and situating contexts, which are drawn upon in this book. But these authoritative narratives tend to focus on what is "known" about the Great Lakes. That tendency is even worse in the realm of land management, where "knowns" are channeled into reactive planning and policy strategies, assuming that people can truly understand complex, dynamic systems and entities and efficiently reconfigure the circumstances to more desirable outcomes. That assumption rarely holds up over greater temporal and spatial scales.

To be clear, this book does not hold a better answer to the question of "what to do." Rather, it hopes to promote the idea that the work of comprehending the Great Lakes Basin should begin and reside intimately with the question of "how to do." As Western colonial development and land management practices have focused on controlling the landscape to achieve desirable outcomes, practitioners have been backed into a corner. The "unknown" and "unpredictable" are viewed as undesirable,

4

dangerous, and scary. These are inherent and highly formative properties of living in this world, but in environmental engineering, planning, and design they are often vilified. We hope to offer a different approach. As designers interested in the past, present, and future of these shorelines, we seek avenues of exploration that allow us to appreciate the dynamism and complexity of this interface, working between the known and the unknown. This book is a record of the methods, findings, stories, and questions of two landscape architecture professors meeting the shorelines of the Great Lake Basin. It is for readers who are familiar with these waters and those who are not. From lichen and hydroelectric dams to perennial grasses and mechanical dredges, this book shares an understanding of the Great Lakes as a region and an experience.

SEEING A WAVE

The opening chapter of Italo Calvino's novel *Mr. Palomar* finds the main character standing on a beach, trying to see a wave. Not *all* waves, mind you. Mr. Palomar wants to observe one individual wave, in all its dimensions, from its rising in the distance to the completion of its action. He considers various aspects of form, pattern, and time that might help isolate a single wave. He even attempts to draw a quadrat on the ocean as a method of measurement. Calvino writes, "If he bears in mind a square zone of, say, ten meters of shore by ten meters of sea, he can carry out an inventory of all the wave movements that are repeated with varying frequency within a given time interval. The hard thing is to fix the boundaries of this zone."[1] Inevitably, Mr. Palomar's field of observation slips. More precisely: "The space under examination is overturned and at the same time crushed." This is a very familiar feeling for an expectant observer. The place between the "known" and the "unknown" is, more often than not, an uncomfortable place to be.

Mr. Palomar's desires do not end there. The reason he wants to see a wave is so that he can then "begin the second phase of the operation: extending this knowledge to the entire universe." But, alas, he does not get that far. Conceding that he will be unable to see the wave, he "goes off along the beach, as tense and nervous as when he came, and even more unsure about everything."[2] Throughout Calvino's book, Mr. Palomar is followed through stages of his futile quest to wholly

5

comprehend the world. He picks at blades of grass, waits in line at a cheese shop, and studies jars of goose fat—always attentive to the materials, forces, and systems that are implicated in the object under consideration. Again and again, Mr. Palomar is frustrated by the limits of human perception; he is unable to escape his own subjectivity. He never feels confident enough to make the leap from experience to universal generalizations. Yet amid his despair there is delight. As he takes on questions about the uncertain depths of humanity and the infinite physical and temporal scales of the universe, Mr. Palomar experiences the frustration of never knowing everything—but also occasionally the satisfaction that comes with getting to know some things better.

LANDSCAPE ARCHITECTURE, PLACE, AND DANCING WITH SYSTEMS

One critical commonality between us as authors, which allows us to share a language, is that we were both educated professionally in the discipline of landscape architecture. By studying and designing landscapes and teaching landscape architecture in American universities, we are part of a relatively young discipline, not much more than a century old, which has a strong European bias and an orientation toward Western culture and property regimes. While this book is not explicitly about what landscape architecture is or how landscape architects work, it does provide a window into how the two of us, from the field of landscape architecture, think about landscapes and how to engage them.

As designers working in and with landscapes, describing "what is" and speculating on "what could be," we revel in the act of getting to know places better. We are not environmental scientists, journalists, or engineers, and we do not devote ourselves to the "art" or "science" of landscape. For us, these ways of thinking are important, but our practice is to find synthetic ways of working that creatively and critically explore the space between them. Instead of claiming authority, purporting facts, and proposing solutions, our efforts are focused on wedging open spatial, ecological, social, and even intellectual systems. Advocating for multiplicitous understandings of place, we try to hold space for more voices, more systems, more species, more times, and feel this is an essential role for our discipline of landscape architecture.

6

As a field, landscape architecture often lies at the fringes of public consciousness. Most often it is colloquially associated with the design of a backyard or park. Indeed, one of the first designers to adopt the title of "landscape architect" and still one of the most famous, Frederick Law Olmsted, was a designer of large parks, including Manhattan's Central Park, Brooklyn's Prospect Park, and many urban park systems across the United States. Less often discussed are Olmsted's other land management efforts, such as the preservation of places like Yosemite and Niagara Falls and the replumbing of Boston's Back Bay, projects that demonstrated the field's agency in the discourses of policy, activism, and urban engineering.

Today what is known as landscape architecture can include the ecological planning of an entire watershed, the design of an urban waterfront, or the arrangement of small elements such as benches or lights. It can involve community engagement methods, landscape sensing/analysis, or the design of landscape management protocols and policies. Landscape architects work with dynamic materials and systems, and their professional skills are relevant across different spatial and temporal scales and varied objectives. Yet the situated and contextual practice of the field helps define it, especially as practitioners and researchers begin to reach beyond mere capitalistic or anthropocentric motives, as they intervene in the physical and spatial stuff of landscape. J. B. Jackson, a landscape architecture professor and writer, defined landscape as "space deliberately created to speed up or slow down the process of nature. . . . It represents man (humans) taking upon himself (themselves) the role of time."[3] Landscape architects thus play a critical role in interrogating, translating, and projecting the possibilities of place within a temporally contingent context.

Understanding a place, though, is not a simple, linear endeavor. Places are complex systems that might benefit from being recognized and celebrated equally for both their familiar and unfamiliar qualities. As Donella Meadows, an environmental systems thinker and physicist, wrote:

> Self-organizing, non-linear, feedback systems are inherently unpredictable. They are not controllable. . . . We can't find a proper, sustainable relationship to nature, each other, or the institutions we

create, if we try to do it from the role of omniscient conqueror. . . .
Systems thinking leads to another conclusion, however—waiting,
shining, obvious, as soon as we stop being blinded by the illusion of
control. It says there is plenty to do, of a different sort of 'doing.' The
future can't be predicted but it can be envisioned and brought lovingly
into being. . . . We can't control systems or figure them out but we
can dance with them![4]

This dance compels us. Both as academics and designers, we are
constantly recalibrating our practice and learning from our landscape
"dance partners." The architect Peter Zumthor wrote that the strength
of "good design" involves "our ability to perceive the world with both
emotion and reason."[5] Emotion and reason here are qualities that
mature as one practices. Design instructors often emphasize the
development of reasoning, which is easily taught and tracked through
conventional modalities of testing, analysis, and representation.
The emotion side of the design process is often trickier to teach and
evaluate, but it is just as essential in the practice of good design. It
might be recognized as the development of one's own intuition based
on expanded contextual fluency. As with any creative process, design
skills are refined through praxis. In landscape architecture, this occurs
both in the craft of making and in the craft of "seeing," particularly in
approaching landscape systems that may never be wholly knowable.
As the author Rebecca Solnit observes in *A Field Guide to Getting Lost*,
the quest for the "unknown" is a way to calibrate oneself.[6] How an
unknown is defined at any given time is a reflection of our previous
findings. It situates our past in relation to our current direction.
Whether speaking of knowns and unknowns, emotion and reason,
or science and art, the dance becomes an instructive metaphor that
guides a good portion of this text as we explore the spaces between the
categories that tend to govern our world.

A GUIDE TO THIS BOOK

Our approach to "seeing" the conditions of the Great Lakes begins
with examination, immersion, interpretation, and the recording our
impressions. One key factor is that the experience and record presented

here are shared between two people. Recognizing this shared aspect is critical to our collaboration and to our work as designers. We are explicitly not trying to speak for anyone but ourselves, as two curious members of the thick collective of participants linked to one of the largest freshwater resources on Earth.[7] Throughout this book, we use the pronoun "we," but not in an attempt to collapse our identities with each other's or anyone else's.[8] Our book, work, explorations, findings, questions—these are all the product of a practice that has emerged between the two of us. We are individuals, with our own collections of memory, experiences, skills, and projected futures, but we approach this work collaboratively, with the idea that our discussions and shared experiences will be informative, challenging, and potentially transformative for the other person. Such recognition is a fundamental component of a collaborative design process, one that honestly recognizes and celebrates subjective differences.

The understandings of place we put forth are not final, concrete, or universal. Our work is always in process, and we are continually developing new methods and learning new ways of emplacement. For now, it is enough to know that this book is a collection of stories about our explorations along the shorelines of the Great Lakes. Naturally, these stories are constructions. Certain conditions and events are elevated; others are suppressed for narrative effect. We do not intend to present our perspectives as "truth," but rather as openly precarious and vulnerable contributions to a larger collective of perspectives.[9] We also recognize that even as we draw from the annals of philosophy throughout this book, we are not philosophy scholars. Our use of these works is not deeply contextualized philosophically; rather, the works are used pragmatically to help us interrogate and expand our methodologies. This process even includes cases where we find the reading of two rather conflicting philosophical positions useful as a way of working through our various approaches of inquiry and description.

Structurally, this book traces our efforts to better know a collection of bay landscapes across the Great Lakes Basin by way of physical experience, experimentation, storytelling, and research. The first chapter, "Toward the Transcalar," examines the role of spatial and temporal scales and how they are used to construct landscape understanding. In this opening chapter, a brief introduction of the Great Lakes history precedes a discussion of the importance of transcalar approaches, and our use of the "bay scale" as a productive transcalar bridge between the regional and experiential scales.

The following series of five chapters then collects our explorations of five different bay landscapes—Saginaw Bay, Nipigon Bay, Green Bay, the Bay of Quinte, and Maumee Bay—one bay for each of the five Great Lakes. Each chapter tracks our explorations of each bay bringing our own experiences together with the observations of others, historical records, numerical data, and memories. These texts, along with our drawings and photographs, can be understood as a gradient of our inquiries documenting our personal understanding of these places, territories, systems, and forces, at particular moments in time.

Interspersed between the bay chapters are a collection of interludes that include interviews and essays by contributors offering up their own critical inquiries of the relationships bound up in this territory. While each contributor comes from a different academic field, one commonality they share is that all are academics housed in institutions within a Great Lakes state. The speakers and authors included here are not responding to the direct material of the book. Rather, they are all responding to the same prompt: to reflect on "change" in the Great Lakes Basin. Each of them was encouraged to interpret this prompt in their own way. For the interviews, we asked follow-up questions based on initial responses, but the conversations were always guided by this reflection on change. These essays and interviews are placed throughout the book, allowing for shifts of voice and consideration. At times they speak indirectly or tangentially to similar conditions or issues, but again, none are speaking directly to any particular bay or to our writings. While these interludes are short, we hope they spur readers to seek out these authors' larger bodies of work.

The first interlude by the biologist Mark Davis, provides a counterpoint to the dominant narrative of biological invasion that has shaped restoration and remediation efforts across the basin. Then, social scientist Mae Davenport shifts the scale of climate change back toward the landscape of Minnesota's North Shore and considers ways to engage local residents. In the third interlude, the geologist Marcia Bjornerud speculates on the potential of thinking with geologic time within the basin. This is followed by an interview with the Indigenous scholar Kyle Powys Whyte in which he discusses his interpretation of changes across the Great Lakes Basin that have produced a highly privatized colonial landscape, under the guise of progress. Lastly, also through an interview, the author and water policy expert Peter Annin casts light on the implications of climate change and water-level fluctuations across a vast region blessed with a tremendous freshwater resource.

After the series of bay exploration chapters and interludes, chapter 7, "Curious Methods," lays out the theoretical framework that undergirds our working methods as site-specific practitioners, explorers, and storytellers. In this final chapter, we make the case for an experiential and experimental practice that advocates for a pluralistic understanding of place, particularly as it relates to the work of design.

A NOTE ON OUR WHITE COLONIAL PERSPECTIVE

In our work within the Great Lakes, we are constantly encountering physical, social, and cultural complexities that call into question what we think we know about the place, and about our roles as educators, designers, and community members. This notably includes recognition of how little we know about the Indigenous and nonwhite history and culture of this place, despite having lived here for much of our lives. Most of the loudest academic narratives of the Great Lakes are produced from a white colonial perspective and they depict and center the activities of colonizers. Museums, libraries, government documents, and online histories have only slivers of information about the Indigenous and other nonwhite residents of the basin in comparison to the histories of colonial settlers and industrial expansion. Bookstores throughout the region contain shelf upon shelf of literature on shipwrecks and lighthouses, but often little about the cataclysmic violence, oppression, marginalization, and fragmentation inflicted upon Indigenous, African American, and other nonwhite people and communities, the history of slavery, inequality, or systemic racism. When genocide is acknowledged, it is depicted as a past event, rather than an ongoing campaign of erasure. White colonialism is pervasive throughout North America, and the Great Lakes region. Almost all

11

the land within the basin is "owned" and "managed" by the colonial regime.

Likewise, colonial systems and colonizing ways of thinking continue to be strong in the institutions of higher education where we were taught, where we ourselves now teach, and within the field of landscape architecture. Indigenous, African American, and other non-white scholars, students, and texts are often marginalized, and systemic racism and inequity are upheld. We cannot change the past nor can we change our identities as white people, but we acknowledge the deep inequities and atrocities that we, as white people in America, are part of and have benefited from. We also look critically at the voices we uphold and amplify, and we are committed to living, learning, teaching, and trying to the best of our abilities to change ourselves and these systems to be more just and equitable.

In our research and practice of this book, concerned with the dynamism of the Great Lakes shorelines and the different ways people might live and design within changing environments, we have notably been introduced to the incredible, powerful, and diverse knowledge shared by many Indigenous scholars.[10] The Métis anthropologist Zoe Todd has noted that while academic theories that decenter humans are growing in popularity—for example, theories on posthumanism and the Anthropocene—many of their intellectual theorizers continue to marginalize the Indigenous perspective.[11] Todd argues that these concepts should be recognized and criticized for their own Eurocentricity; they assume universal perspectives and overlook or disregard significant and preexisting Indigenous scholarship and histories.

We acknowledge the strengths of the Indigenous framework and seek to understand it better while recognizing our inherent privileges, biases, Western colonial tendencies, and that we are not immune to Todd's critique. We heed Todd's offering of a critical approach from the Papaschase Cree scholar Dwayne Donald, who proposes a concept of *ethical relationality*, "the ethical imperative to see that despite our varied place-based cultures and knowledge systems, we live in the world together and must constantly think and act with reference to those relationships."[12] We strive, as Donald proposes, to better "orient" ourselves to an "ethic of historical consciousness," recognizing that "the past occurs simultaneously in the present and influences

12

how we conceptualize the future . . . Any knowledge we gain about the world interweaves us more deeply with these relationships, and gives us life."[13] As we begin this book, we thank all who have shared their knowledge with us directly and indirectly, and we recognize that we are still in the constant process of learning and growing. We acknowledge that the lands and waters where we grew up, from which we are learning, and where our work has taken place are the traditional homelands of many Indigenous communities, including the Potawatomi, Métis, Anishinabewaki, Sioux, Menominee, Miami, Peoria, Odawa, Sauk, Attiwonderonk, Huron-Wendat, Algonquin, St. Lawrence Iroquoians, Haudenosaunee, Onundagaonoga, Wenrohronon, Seneca, Erie, Fox, Lenni Lenape, and Delaware, most all of which include more localized tribes, bands, and nations.[14]

FIGURE 1.1. Western Basin of Lake Erie. View of the blue-green algae bloom in the Western Basin of Lake Erie as seen from the Landsat 8 Satellite on July 30, 2019. Image: NASA Earth Observatory.

I

TOWARD THE TRANSCALAR

PERHAPS THE MOST DRAMATIC IMAGES OF THE GREAT LAKES published in the past decade were taken by NASA. From space, the satellite captures a huge bright-green splotch growing in summer months on the surface of Lake Erie. The spread of ancient microscopic Cyanobacteria, an event commonly known as "algae bloom," now regularly threatens to contaminate the water supply of cities such as Toledo, Ohio; and beaches are closed due to its toxicity to animals and people. This photosynthetic bacterium is so small that it cannot be removed with a mesh, and yet its colonies grow so large and so bright that they can be seen by a satellite orbiting hundreds of miles above Earth. To understand how the algae growth is linked to seasonal pulses from massive farming operations and to landscape management methods that leach nitrogen and phosphorus into the waterways, one must zoom across scales of time and operation. From the visceral bodily sickness this organism can cause to international food systems of the fields, algae blooms offer a prime example of the importance and need for using multiple scales of awareness and action when considering the environmental, ecological, and social issues of the future Great Lakes. Setting aside the satellite and the microscope, one's actual experience of such a bloom is itself a notable happening. Imagine puttering along in a boat across water that more aptly resembles a thick pea soup. The gentle winds cause the surface of the verdant mass to ripple like a piece of fabric as the brightness, viscosity, and looming toxicity make the scene almost otherworldly and untouchable.

Any serious landscape inquiry or intervention has always dealt with issues of scale. Scale is used to define and organize conditions and is foundational to the framing of problems. It is likewise tied to human experience, methods and tools of observation, the recognition of patterns, and communication. Consideration of scale is not new, but as the architectural educator Adrian Lahoud has noted, "New kinds of problems—like climate change, for instance—pose special challenges insofar as they bring together the large and the small, the near and the far, the fast and the slow, the weak and the strong, making a mess of existing scalar conventions."[1] Indeed, the mess of scales has only become messier and more complex as many anthropogenic systems continue to grow larger and move faster. Consider the analogy of attempting to loosen a ball of tangled string. Beginning with a singular strand, pulling at one or even a series of strings individually feels like the obvious approach, but these singular acts only tighten the ball elsewhere, making the tangle more difficult to resolve. And yet any attempt to address the whole entity as a ball, say hitting it with a hammer or shaking it in frustration, completely overlooks its construction and likewise is unhelpful. What is needed is a concerted effort that shifts between individual strings and the ball as a whole, patiently loosening it up over time until you can work your fingers into it. For us, finding ways of working our fingers into the landscapes of the Great Lakes Basin requires the constant and concurrent cognition and use of multiple scales—that is, a "transcalar" approach.

Before we begin tossing this ball around though, let us linger for a moment on some of the dominant scales of space and time at play. While subjects may be observed at multiple scales, all cannot be comprehended at the same time. As Peter Harries-Jones notes, following Gregory Bateson: "If all is in flux, and everything is changing and

▶ FIGURE 1.2. Algae across Scales. From the microscopic to the regional, algae is a formidable actor in the Great Lakes landscape, one that is tied to both experience of place and large-scale planning efforts. Image by the authors.

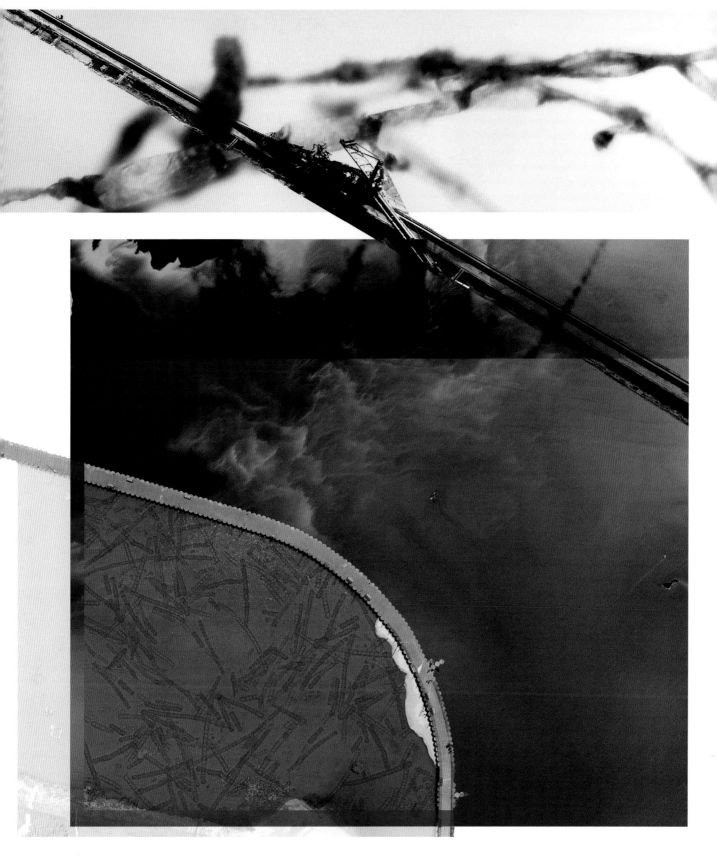

nothing remains the same, then it is difficult for the observers, who are also changing, to construct any point of reference."[2] To deal with constant change, it is necessary to establish temporary (and therefore deceptive) points of reference so that patterns, relationships, or *patterns of relationships* can be recognized.[3] Therefore, landscape is only ever partially understood, but establishing points and scales of reference is critical, even if they are temporary. Not surprisingly, the reference points from which we can work continue to expand. Extreme spatial scales, for example, have only recently been perceivable by humans. With the invention of the microscope in the sixteenth century, people began to see and understand microbes and cellular structures, a technology that continues to develop today. And while summited mountain peaks have long provided expansive views, and triangulation methods have allowed for precise surveying methods, the first aerial photographs were taken by balloon only in the mid-nineteenth century. People can now study the Earth from Mars, and particle physicists continue to find new nested scales of matter, thus making it possible to consider systems from the cosmic to the quantum. With all these possible perspectives, it becomes essential to mix and incorporate a range of strategies in order to genuinely explore this "mess." For the Great Lakes, we will begin with the large planimetric view of the five major lakes, a scale that is depicted across bumper stickers and T-shirts, and that tends to dominate the discussion of this region.

THE GREAT (BIG) LAKES

As its name implies, the Great Lakes Basin is popularly defined by its immense scale. The 5,000 cubic miles of water collected here amounts to roughly 20 percent of the world's surficial freshwater supply. There are over 10,000 miles of shoreline and more than 30 million people living in a drainage area that covers 200,000 square miles of land. These statistics are used by land managers, politicians, journalists, and everyone else to emphasize the Great Lakes' economic, social, and ecological value. "The basin is big" = *the basin is important*. The large scale is an identifier that brings fame and notoriety, allowing the Great Lakes to compete for attention (and resources) with other regions of North America. These are the "Sweet Seas," in the parlance of colonial explorers, or, more recently, the "Third Coast" or "North Coast."

Although each lake and its associated subbasin is unique, the lakes are elementally connected by the water they share. These waters have supported Indigenous nations for thousands of years, well before the arrival of the European explorers and colonial settlers 350 years ago. This arrival was followed by an amplification of resource extraction beginning with the trading of furs and harvesting of wood, which drove significant development across the shorelines. The same could be said about many North American landscapes, but the "scaling up" of development and urbanism across the basin in the nineteenth and twentieth centuries was unprecedented. The urban planner and historian Robert Fishman goes so far as to argue that from 1860 to 1960, "the Great Lakes Megaregion was the most productive and innovative place on earth."[4] This productivity reflected a convergence of new transportation and production technologies in a resource-rich region. The nodes, connections, and relationships established by fur traders and loggers provided ideal conduits for the rapid growth of new industries.

This era of expansion—or "progress"—involved shifts in temporal and spatial scales across multiple domains, including human move-ment, communication, and industrial action. Collectively, these shifts supported changes toward what the philosopher Bruno Latour and others call the "Global." Latour writes that with the desire to be "mod-ern," much of society has strapped itself onto an airplane heading to-ward a global positioning, "which aroused enthusiasm for generations because it was synonymous with wealth, freedom, knowledge, and access to a life of ease." The "Local" and the "Anti-Global," filled with old certainties and traditions, had to be left behind.[5] And so within a century or so, fueled by these desires of the global and the modern, the Great Lakes was transformed, underpinning much of the physical and experiential conditions found across the basin today.

Due to swiftness and timing, the Great Lakes Basin was one of the first regions where the scale of the spatial, ecological, and economic effects of progress could be registered, and where, too, it was disguised. Growth outpaced disaster. Chicago, for example, grew by 60 percent during the same decade (the 1870s) in which a fire burned nearly a third of the city to the ground. The booming regional economy funded ambitious city planning and development efforts all across the basin. In 1893, Chicago entered the world stage by hosting the World's Columbian Exposition. And by the early 1900s, many Great Lakes cities such as Duluth, Minnesota, were positioning themselves to be the "New York City" of the Midwest. It may seem hard to believe now, but such claims had justification in their day. By 1910, four of the country's ten largest cities were tucked next to a Great Lake. Elaborate plans were followed by major investments in parks and other infrastructure. Frederick Law Olmsted, the most famous landscape architect in the country at the time, was recruited to design parks and parkways systems in many of these cities, including Chicago, Milwaukee, Detroit, and Buffalo.

In a well-known history, this growth in the late 1800s and early 1900s set the stage for the Rust Belt conditions that followed, when cities in the Great Lakes saw their economies and populations shrink dramatically. One famous example is Detroit, which quadrupled in size between 1910 and 1950 to a peak population of 1.85 million. The city scaled up its infrastructure accordingly, building new roads and neighborhoods to accommodate workers for growing companies such as the auto giants Ford, General Motors, and Chrysler. But when manufacturing declined in the 1960s along with the growth of social and political unrest, those neighborhoods began to empty out almost as quickly as they had filled. Detroit's population in 2019 was about 670,000. In similar trends, both Buffalo and Cleveland have lost over 40 percent of their populations since the 1950s. Throughout the region, complex social and economic factors resulted in suburbanization and outmigration to less urban areas. As factories ceased production and downtowns emptied out, their infrastructure became overscaled for their usage and suffered from a lack of maintenance and care. Abandoned homes on oversized roads could not sustain a supportive tax base. Social and economic inequities grew, and mobility became a luxury for those who could afford it. These conditions have been in place, and in some cases worsening, for three generations. And while the residue of shrinkage still coats these cities, the decline cannot be attributed to the region as a whole, for while people left the urban centers, they spurred the growth of adjacent suburban communities.

Despite the Rust Belt designation, the regional population of the Great Lakes has actually been growing continually. Change is, of course, a matter of scale.

The growth of this region called for land management policies and priorities that could transgress the abstract borders between countries, states, tribal lands, and other applied administrative edges, including a multinational negotiation of environmental protections and recommendations rarely afforded to other bodies of water. The International Joint Commission, established by the 1909 Boundary Waters Treaty between Canada and the United States, was initially developed to "prevent and resolve disputes over the use of the waters" such as those posed by growing hydroelectric power infrastructure and shipping within the Great Lakes.[6] In the middle of the twentieth century, its mandate was expanded to include investigating water and air quality issues and making policy recommendations at the basin scale. Meanwhile, the actual management of environmental change is left to other organizations, including the US Environmental Protection Agency, Environment and Climate Change Canada, and state Departments of Natural Resources, Departments of Sewage and Water Treatments, NOAA (National Oceanic and Atmospheric Administration) Sea Grants, and many local interest groups.

Suffice it to say that many of the identified environmental, ecological, and social issues facing the Great Lakes are understood, discussed, and negotiated at the large regional level, recognizing the repercussions of localized behaviors. For many who live here, the silhouette of the five lakes has become a symbol of home or a call to awareness and action for the waters. Indeed, this regional vantage point is critical to landscape planning as it relates to and influences specific tools of environmental management and assessment, geopolitics, legal regimes, climate change, and so forth. However, a focus on these larger scales also perpetuates many of these same issues, demanding more large-scale regional attention, often at the detriment of unique attributes, qualities, and experience of place. While planning efforts often recommend the "future" incorporation of more local, contextual idiosyncrasies of place, in practice the local and experiential concerns are often lost to "efficient" one-size-fits-most approaches. No matter how well intentioned or eyeopening, it should never be

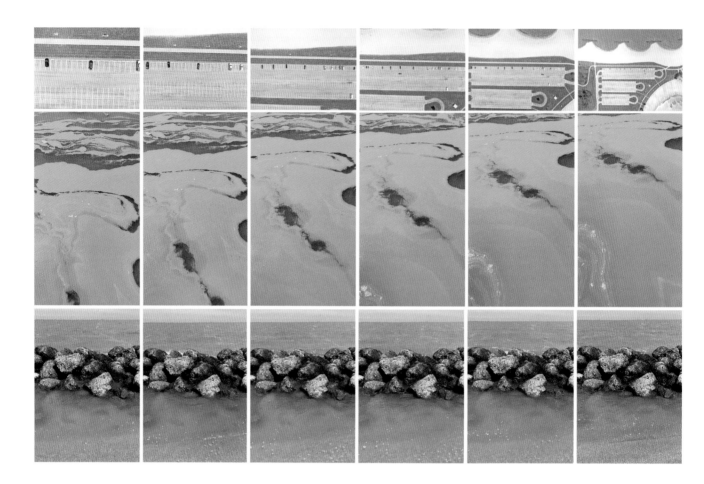

FIGURE 1.3. Shifting Scales: From Ground to Air. Images composed from various perspectives and across time along the shoreline of Maumee Bay. As waves lap against a breakwater or algae slide over the water's surface, how these happenings are understood is a product of perspective. Image by the authors.

forgotten that mapping at the large scale originates in Western colonial conquests and territorial claims that championed (and continue to champion) growth and exploitation. Tools and data sets designed to visualize or analyze regional issues such as sediment budgets, wetland loss, or biodiversity require normalization across a vast range of local conditions, producing generalizations that overwrite much of what made those conditions local in the first place. It is necessary to simultaneously consider other scales beyond the regional if these local conditions are to be preserved or valued.

THE BODY

One particularly strong counterpoint to the top-down gaze of the regional level is found in the scale of experience and embodiment. At this scale, we find ourselves sitting on a dock swatting at mosquitoes or overeating at an all-you-can-eat perch fish fry. Whether we are excited, exhausted, bored, hot, freezing, restless, or (of course) curious, our bodies, memories, thoughts, and actions are bound to unique locations and relations. Similar to the large scale, the extents of these more intimate small scales are ambiguous and variable. They are also influential and formative. And this embodied scale is intimately tied to our senses. Recognizing our bodies as constant sensors—feeling, smelling, listening, tasting, touching, conceiving, recording, responding, and changing—this scale allows us to explore how we both form and inform the environment around us. As the philosopher Henri Lefebvre stated, "Each living body produces itself in space and simultaneously produces that space."[7] The scale of the body, and the space and relationships derived from that scale, matter. Every body within the Great Lakes Basin, all thirty-plus million of them, is an agent of change, a space-maker, through their actions at the experiential scale—whether they choose (or are permitted) to acknowledge this or not. To go further, the process of sensing is in no way unidirectional nor is it a solely human endeavor, as the relationships we experience are experienced by others. The anthropology professor Natasha Myers, who uses sensing in her work, in this case within an oak savanna, describes her approach as the "very questioning of what it means to pay attention to all these beings who have been paying attention."[8] Indeed, the mistaken idea that the experiential is merely a personal endeavor, devoid of social or collective agency, sorely overlooks the responsibility we all have in our everyday actions and experiences.

Experience itself is something that could be understood as the felt processes of transition or, as the human geographer Derek McCormack writes, a "field of variation"; and by way of "experimenting"

23

with experience we can "multiply the forces, events and processes that we admit as participants in this perplexing matter of worldly involvement."[9] Working and thinking at this scale provides a way in, to reach these more manifold and rich experiences. As we will discuss in a somewhat different context in chapter 7, what is particularly interesting to us is how we may *thicken* those experiences. These thick experiences are "reconstructed" from previous experiences and memories in a way that could even be painful.[10] As new experiences are folded or cut into previous ones, they create something altogether new and yet ultimately meaningful. But as a single thick collection, as perceived by one body, the experiential scale continues to be dismissed by decision makers and is often unable to be part of the greater dialogue or design response. The typical argument is that experiences are too temporary, small, and uncertain, and they lack the "objectivity" to make them truly effective at the scale of design and planning.

What could be useful here to give more credence and criticality to the experiential scale and its possibilities as a strategic bundling of thick experiences into a collective of voices. As the philosopher Donna Haraway states in her argument for "situated knowledges" and "Feminist objectivity," "the only way to find a larger vision is to be somewhere in particular."[11] Here she recognizes the importance of "communities" over the "individual" as the relationships and exchanges of community allow for the "situation" of criticality and collective participation. In addition to the collective, we believe that the ability for the experiential scale to be in discussion with greater regional issues could also be helpful. Working in this way could be seen as an active process of *middling* that is not necessarily about landing between scales, but instead about continually working between them, pulling from both ends in an effort to acknowledge the values of each while working to ensure that one is never dominant. This is assisted by the idea that these two "ends" are tethered to one another from the start, that what we experience is already socially and politically situated. Experience is, as the human geographers Kirsten Simonsen and Lass Koefoed write, "already infused with layers of cultural sedimentation, saturated with habit and inertia, and interwoven with power and obfuscation, that it must be ceaselessly interrogated and opened up to experiments."[12] So, there is a middle ground here, one that we, along

24

FIGURE 1.4. Atmospheric Transects. A transect across a cobble beach on the Nipigon Bay provides an opportunity to see the scale and patterns created by littoral processes and how, when mixed with atmospheric conditions like fog, they create specific and memorable experiences. Image by the authors.

with other practitioners in design and planning, are aiming for in our own ways; a path where local thinking and action can co-construct the regional as a plurality of perspectives. We might also consider this process a search for a method of transcalar work, one that can effectively and actively fold experience into larger regional objectives. This mode of practice moves beyond "thinking global and acting local" and necessitates a "thinking local" that places value on individual places and experiences, even while considering regional challenges. As regions are considered from above and decisions are made about how to act, there can also be space for the local specificities to push back and inform the process. Striking a balance here requires an exercise in transcalar thinking and action and a commitment to engaging the mess.

IN SEARCH OF A TRANSCALAR LANDSCAPE

> When the rug is pulled out from under your feet, you understand at once that you are going to have to be concerned with the floor."
>
> —Bruno Latour, *Down to Earth*

We cannot simply choose a scale and assume it will reveal answers. Every scale is at once too large and too small, too fast and too slow, too broad and too narrow to perceive the true intricacies of a situation. In light of this, we hold particular appreciation for transcalar approaches. In *Down to Earth*, Bruno Latour illuminates the tremendous difficulties associated with scale, as they relate to the politics of living in and with the world. Latour identifies society's current position as somewhere between the "attractors" of the "Global" and the "Local," and he describes a third attractor—the "Terrestrial"—which may help negotiate the tension between these two poles. Terrestrial here describes the interrelated agents of a particular earthbound context: humans, soil bacteria, forests, other animals, and so on. Accordingly, thinking through the terrestrial involves a shift in focus from "production" to "engendering"; Latour suggests that people must see themselves as distributed, dependent occupants of a specific place. He further argues that "we are not seeking agreement from all these overlapping agents but learning to be dependent on them. *No reduction, no harmony*."[13]

26

People must recognize and insert themselves into lineages of other agents. To be "engendering" other terrestrials, living and nonliving, must be accounted for and humans must equitably consider their own trajectories and interests.[14] Latour proposes this method of engendering as a considered response to the anthropocentric hubris, inequality, and climate concerns of the present era.

Donna Haraway describes human interdependent relations with other beings as a sympoiesis, or a "making with." She reminds us that "nobody lives everywhere and everybody lives somewhere, nothing is connected to everything and everything is connected to something."[15] We are all bodies that turn to compost. Instead of attempting to move past a moment of ecological crisis toward a technological, posthuman future, Haraway advocates "staying with the trouble." This involves making connections or "kin" with all organisms, human and nonhuman alike. It also requires thinking across multiple scales, physical and temporal, in ways that are messy and indeterminate; considering beyond our own lifetimes and our own subjectivity. Both Latour and Haraway imagine a way of working that acknowledges the transcalar relationships with other beings and times within a particular spatial context.

Such powers of recognition, however, are seldom achieved. More often, decision makers, whether they are politicians, engineers, planners, designers, or the like, find scales to be problematic or contradictory. Since management roles and positions are often locked into perceiving the world through the scales they are comfortable with or have control over, decisions are often myopic, reactionary, and disconnected. Nuisance scales are often ignored, discredited, or recast. Many assume the power to "command and control" environmental conditions without regard for the interests of actors outside of a capitalist, anthropogenic perspective.[16] Such habits are seen today across the shoreline management of the Great Lakes. Land managers, hamstrung by the limitations of their positions, expectations, and constituents, seem unable to operate within a transcalar agenda. This agenda would incorporate local sites, sediment sheds, nonhuman species habitat, regional concerns, and climate shifts, instead of making decisions based on short-term enjoyment, political cycles, or the presumed predictability of the coastal environment. The challenge is to see past political borders and recognize that the water, the land, the animals, and the plants are not bound to ownership. Rather, these shared systems influence one another—something often missed by the pouring of concrete seawalls or the replacing of marsh conditions with neatly mowed grass. Similarly, temporal scales like water residence time or nonhuman lifespans are ignored when making decisions that are biased toward human production. Discovering ways of practicing while acknowledging the aforementioned considerations is a tremendous challenge but it should be among our most pressing goals.

Consider the blackpoll warbler (*Setophaga striata*), a bird that spends the winter in the South American Andes and the summer in the Canadian boreal forest. As the warbler makes its way across the continent, it migrates through the Great Lakes Basin, expecting to find food and rest in "scrubby thickets and mature evergreen and deciduous forests."[17] Each individual bird, small enough to fit in the palm of a hand, requires habitat that encompasses thousands of miles and decades of growth. The warbler is not bound by the politics of landownership, but it is affected by them, entangled within them, as it tries to find food and clean water, and avoid wind turbines and house cats.

With some intention and research, a person can think through the scales that are important to the warbler, superimposing its migratory route and seasonal habits on the location of parks and backyards. People can commit to follow and expand upon climate adaptation plans such as one developed in 2016 by the 1854 Treaty Authority in which the needs of resident species are anticipated beyond boundary lines to better assist their survival through current climate change projections.[18] But how can all scales and all other beings be considered simultaneously? They simply cannot. What can be done, though, is to develop ways of synthesizing and prioritizing information that give credence to scales and systems of interdependence, while acknowledging the limits of predictability and certainty. Closer attention can also be paid to the spatial and temporal scales that are seldom heard or studied, that are omitted or erased by the processes of generalization and classification that decision making requires.

The ecological turn in landscape practice has made the terms "resilience" and "adaptability" quite popular in recent decades. While these concepts are often misused, they are powerful frameworks for recognizing the transience of natural systems and the unknowability of new inputs and forces. Ecological "resilience" was introduced in a 1973 paper by C. S. Holling, who argued that ecology's analytic methods were unduly influenced by other disciplines. They tended to be quantitative rather than qualitative, and they narrowed the scales of observation to focus on a "static state" or "stability," which caused many ecologists to miss the importance of dynamic fluctuations within a system and external factors without. "Natural systems have a high capacity to absorb change without dramatically altering," Holling wrote. "But this resilient character has its limits, and when the limits are passed . . . the system rapidly changes."[19]

Holling proposed studying resilience by using an exercise that considers the survival of a specific species. From this perspective, ecologists could look across scales of time and space to understand the factors influencing an environment (a shift in temperature and climate, the introduction of a new predator, etc.) and observe their relationship to the subject species. Resilience in this case is a measure of the species' ability to adapt to changes to the ecosystem by changing behaviors or tolerances. "A management approach based on resilience," Holling concludes, "would emphasize the need to *keep options open*, the need to view events in a regional rather than a local context, and the need to emphasize heterogeneity. Flowing from this would be not the presumption of sufficient knowledge, but the recognition of ignorance; not the assumption that future events are expected, but that they will be unexpected."[20] Theories of resilience and adaptability have similarly appeared in studies of social and economic systems.[21] Whereas "change" in ecology often points toward the extinction of a species, the "change" factor when discussing the resilience of other systems is not always negative. Change can be positive or merely different. Recognizing "change" as a constant can reduce energy wasted in efforts of pure resistance.

A transcalar approach empowers individual and community values to compete with greater societal values (e.g., capitalism) and physical realities (which may be temporary). In many cases, this means retrieving contextual information that can push back against global or high-level generalizations and categories. For example, as mentioned early in this chapter, people often assume that the population decline experienced by many Great Lakes cities has affected the entire region, urban or not. The badge of decline provides justification for a litany of urban renewal projects, tax abatement schemes, and social engineering experiments targeted at the urban anthropological scale; many of which have social and racial underpinnings. A genuine consideration of the human and nonhuman effects of sprawl elsewhere in the region may produce alternative possibilities. Local habitat restoration will fail if it does not consider basin-wide climate shifts, just as regional efforts have the ability to undermine a local sense of place. Clearly a transcalar approach is warranted, but what exactly might such a method look like?

For a simple first example, take the "watershed unit," a mapping method that operates like a telescope allowing for the shift between scales. All around the Great Lakes, watersheds marked by ridgelines of varied intensities collect water and tip their lands down to rivers and the lakes. Topography provides a context-dependent system for navigating landscape scales from the catchment area of the entire basin to the small tributaries that feed individual lakes. In this way, the use of simple topography can serve as a type of transcalar method of understanding. Sometimes it is more useful to explore between scales than within them. Gregory Bateson's approach to establishing connections through patterns provides a type of working method. Bateson describes this as looking for "patterns which connect," and he encourages us to focus on "similar relations between parts. Never quantities, always shapes, forms, and relations."[22] Identifying patterns and meta-patterns requires breaking the bounding scale. Things that appear disparate and disconnected become related and recognized when observed across spatial and temporal scales, thus highlighting relationships and patterns as transcalar tools.

A compelling example of how this form of transcalar thinking could be leveraged by designers to potentially influence decision making comes by way of the landscape architect Jane Wolff.[23] In her book and project *Delta Primer*, Wolff interrogates the large region of the California Delta, where the Sacramento and San Joaquin Rivers meet the San Francisco Bay. In an attempt to reconcile the contested histories of land use, infrastructure, and cultural values, *Delta Primer* is organized as a type of card game, allowing for the rather serendipitous entanglements of various actors within the region, forcing a consideration of their relationships and potential collective agency. The "suits" of the primer's card deck are organized as "Garden," "Machine," "Wilderness," and "Toy" as a way to categorize and visualize forces ranging from a small dredge to a mass of migrating shorebirds. *Delta Primer* straddles the boundary between design and planning, where creative and experiential acts of drawing and projection encourage new ways of reconsidering how we make decisions at the regional scale.

TIME AS TRANSCALAR METHOD

> Trees are remarkable dancers. You just have to slow down your sense of time to keep pace with the rush of their agile, moving bodies.
>
> —Natasha Myers, "Ungrid-able Ecologies"

One way of addressing the chasm between the regional and the very specific could come by way of temporal thinking. When time is considered at all, often only the short term is recognized, because we now live in a world where power is derived from short-term reckonings.[24] This stunted perspective does not sync with the longer timescales of climate change and the nonhuman world. In *The Mushroom at the End of the World*—a meditation "on the possibility of life in capitalist ruins"—Anna Lowenhaupt Tsing writes, "Progress is a forward march, drawing other kinds of time into its rhythms. Without that driving beat, we might notice other temporal patterns. Each living thing remakes the world through seasonal pulses of growth, lifetime reproductive patterns, and geographies of expansion."[25] As Tsing observes, "growth" is only one part of a lifecycle. The "reproductive patterns" and "seasonal pulses" that surround us also deserve attention and require the prioritization of different rhythms.

The philosopher Michel Serres has attributed the widening disconnect between humans and natural phenomena to the increasing share of time that is spent indoors. In *The Natural Contract*, he notes that in French the word "temps" means both "time" and "weather." Yet our present non-weather-dependent condition has separated the two terms and allowed for the creation of two different times—that of the indoor, short-term decision maker and the outdoor, subservient "peasant" or "sailor" whose life is linked with the weather. We may notice as we walk outside that the leaves have fallen and are collecting on the ground, but we do not watch closely or long enough to see the whole event: the leaves slowly changing color, drying up, and falling. The indoor time of politicians, scientists, and media workers (Serres's list of decision makers) does not relate to the long-term systems they are attempting to manage.[26] And the hegemony of indoor time has largely eradicated deep memories, traditions, instinct, and the accumulated experiences of cultures that are unable to defend themselves against it.

Serres's weather time references a type of long anthropological temporality, but there are other, even slower timescales also worth our consideration. The geologist Marcia Bjornerud, a contributor to this book, argues that our society is "temporally illiterate" and that we have no sense for the "temporal proportion" of Earth's history.[27] For many thousands of years, humans did not have the technology to read that deep history. That has changed now, with advancements in earth science, but most people still seem to ignore geological timescales, even if seeing deep patterns of environmental change would help us understand the natural consequences of our actions. In an evocative passage, Bjornerud describes the awakening of geology students who begin to understand that "rocks are not nouns but verbs—visible evidence of processes: a volcanic eruption, the accretion of a coral reef, the growth of a mountain belt."[28]

Developing the capability to see across timescales could help us conceive future possibilities within systems of vast unpredictability. The debate in 1922 between the theoretical physicist Albert Einstein and the philosopher Henri Bergson might guide our thinking here.[29] For Einstein, the world was calculable, and time, in theory, was reversible. Constants such as the speed of light could be used to precisely calculate temporal events, producing objective facts on which future theories could be built. And, indeed, many of Einstein's theories have been corroborated by advanced methods of observation and measurement. Bergson, however, believed that time (which he eventually referred to as "duration") was thicker, more complex, and experiential. Time was lived, not measured, and its one-way trajectory permitted the development of novelty through a process he called "creative evolution." He saw time and change as tightly related, almost synonymous. Change happens to things through time; this is the fundamental law that underpins all else. And because change happens to things, gripping and molding them, change *creates* things, making new forms out of the continually shifting mix of past and present.[30] Bergson valued time not just as lived experience but as a creative force.

This consideration of time as "creative" alludes to time having agency or purpose. And while this opens intriguing possibilities for design and planning, the agency of time can also be explored in its use as a weapon of control and subjugation. The weaponization of time is framed distinctly by the cultural theorist Brittney Cooper in a TED talk, "The Racial Politics of Time."[31] Cooper lays out the role of time in perpetuating systemic racism, stating bluntly that "time is owned by white people." For example, she explains how stereotypes of "lateness" are used to demonstrate the failings of African American peoples within white supremacy. Mark Rifkin has similarly elucidated how time is weaponized against Indigenous people in the unending processes of colonization.[32] These examples illustrate two important points and avenues for action. First is the need to "dismantle" the clockwork of those in power by exposing the ways time is discretely used for violence and control.[33] Second is the simple acknowledgment that time *does* something, whether that is measuring, interpreting, or subjugating. It should not be assumed that time is objectively experienced and innocently devoid of agency.

Thinking beyond the human timeline is necessary to become temporally "literate," as Bjornerud puts it. Whether it is geologic time, expressed in millions of years, or the brief lifespan of a mayfly, measured in hours, there is value in considering slow and fast timescales that are hard to register within human experiences. Tsing likewise reminds us that by deliberately suppressing the beat of progress, we can better hear other temporal patterns. Fluctuation, migration, evolution: these processes are not only spatial but temporal. Moving between weather time, geological time, nonhuman time, and a time of creative evolution is a critical part of developing the transcalar or scale-jumping abilities that could support more successful, equitable, and meaningful landscape practices.

33

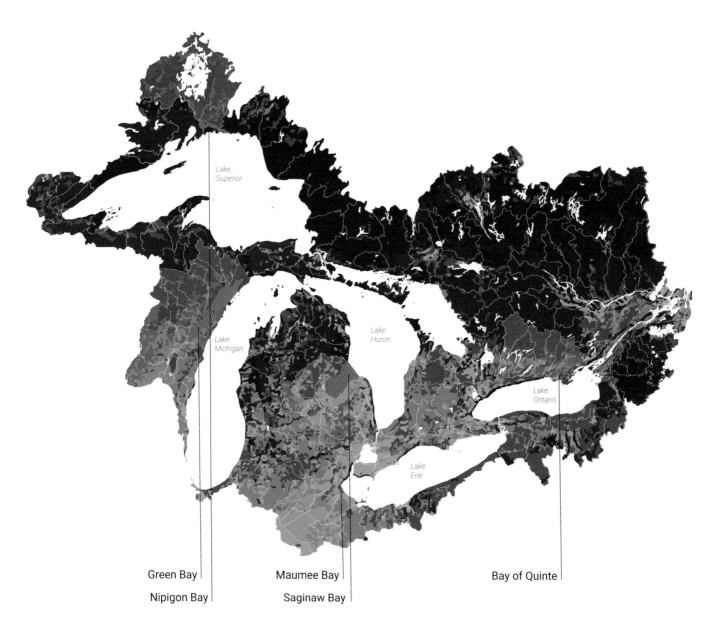

Green Bay

Nipigon Bay

Maumee Bay

Saginaw Bay

Bay of Quinte

FIGURE I.5. Basins and Bays. Watersheds of the Great Lakes Basin and the five bays that are explored in this text (in orange), including their associated drainage areas (in brown). Image by the authors.

Yet all this fluctuation and shifting makes it hard to land anywhere—
something that is essential if the aforementioned concerns are to be taken
seriously. With this consideration, we began to home in on the "bay
scale," In the bay scale, we have found the space between multinational
regulation, regional management and control, and the mud between our
toes. The United Nations Convention on the Law of the Sea defines a
bay as "an indentation that constitutes more than a mere curvature of the
coast where its area is as large as, or larger than, that of the semi-circle
whose diameter is a line drawn across the mouth of that indentation."[34]
This regulatory definition, however, does little to capture what a bay
actually *is* beyond its planimetric geography. The Great Lakes Water
Quality Agreement recognized bays as distinct places that are uniquely
sensitive to changes in water quality within a much larger hydrological
system—highlighting one of the unique qualities of the "bay" scale.
Open to the greater body of water, but formed in such a way that allows
for a concentration of water and sediment, the bay becomes a useful
scale-shifting step down from the regional toward something more
experientially meaningful. For us, the bay becomes our "terrestrial."

The Great Lakes Water Quality Agreement, originally signed
in 1972 and amended in 1983, 1987, and 2012, established forty-three
high-priority areas known as Areas of Concern (AOCs), where
"significant impairment of beneficial uses has occurred as a result of
human activities at the local level."[35] Under the agreement, Remedial
Action Plans were developed in an effort to clean up and eventually
"delist" these places. As of fall 2021, there were still thirty-four active
AOCs, including five discussed in this book: the Saginaw River and
Bay, the Fox River (lower Green Bay), Nipigon Bay, the Bay of Quinte,
and the Maumee River and Bay. Each of these locations (and many
of the other AOCs) occur within shallow embayments (bays), where
kinks in the shoreline provide a semisheltered area.[36] These are also
often associated with a river mouth, which provides an opportunity for
water-based pollutants from upriver to concentrate at the river's end.

The bay is a moment in a greater system, distinguished by its
sheltered topography, comparatively small volume of water, and large
inputs from local rivers. It responds quickly to shifts in wind and

temperature. And since there is less water to dissipate sediment or contaminants, environmental reactions to such inputs are often quicker and more visible than in other parts of the Great Lakes. Since bays are both more easily contaminated *and* more easily monitored, it is not surprising that so many were designated as Areas of Concern. This status encouraged governments and other actors to devote more resources to their study and management, and consequently bays have some of the best observed and best documented shorelines in the basin. This reality is encouraging as it underscores the bay scale as one of considerable importance, in terms of both analysis and action. We too believe that the bay provides a forum for this much-needed localized systemic thinking located between scales. As climate change intensifies, it is crucial that landscape designers and managers become adept at thinking through and across scales to respond to unprecedented and unimaginable conditions "within the accelerated reshuffling of just about everything."[37]

On an experiential level, the small scale of the bay enables a unique perspective. The nearness of the opposite shore allows an observer to visually register the water as part of the formation; thus, "bay" is both water and land. The smaller size also makes it easier to travel across the unit in one day, thus tightening the temporal scale. And yet bays are large enough to encompass a variety of land uses and owners. The bay is not a singular site, but a landscape that tells regional stories, which are relevant throughout the entire basin. In our explorations, we used the bays as stepping-stones, or points of negotiation, between the scale of the Great Lakes Basin and the scale of the site, with its material conditions and inherent ephemeralities. The bay scale allows an observer to see patterns that echo across the ten thousand miles of Great Lakes shorelines. The bay reveals both site-specific and basin-general details.

This book is a record of our attempts to *see* the bay. To understand a thing, we must assemble pieces of contextual information and work to recognize similarities and differences as part of working with the "patterns that connect." With technology, we can, as Shannon Mattern writes, "sense almost any space in the world, from deep sea trenches to the chambers of the human heart," observing connections and influences across a multiscalar universe—but that does not change the nature of the basic operation.[38] We cannot escape the subjectivity of the human body and its senses, mind, and spirit. All our tools, observations, imaginations, and communications are bound to that perspective.

Within this book, we tell the story of our efforts to "meet" five different bays in the Great Lakes Basin. In choosing these five bays, we established a loose set of rules. Each bay would be on a different lake, and each would be situated at the mouth of a river linking the lake to a terrestrial watershed. (This condition is common to most bays, although there are exceptions like Erie's Presque Isle Bay and the Georgian Bay.) Further, each would be designated as an Area of Concern by the Great Lakes Water Quality Agreement, indicating that "significant impairment of beneficial uses have occurred as a result of human activities at the local level."[39] We included bays that we both already knew well, such as Green Bay in Wisconsin, Saginaw in Michigan, and Maumee Bay in Ohio, and bays that we had seldom visited, like Nipigon Bay and the Bay of Quinte. This allowed us to explore new places as first-time visitors, with eyes wide open, while also encouraging the mining of memories, research, and experiences that come with time and repeat visits.

The discipline of landscape architecture has a long tradition of visual communication for both contextual analysis and projective possibilities. Our work here is the product of site investigation and data collection and takes the form of both text-based descriptions and visual imagery—a series of "impressions."[40] These hybrid textual/visual products allow us to think through and communicate particular patterns and relationships *in time*, as we grapple with the messy coastal conditions we encounter. Instead of distilling or oversimplifying these conditions, we aim to illuminate the agency and effects these changing landscapes have on *us*. They are, of course, aesthetic as they are tethered to experience, meant to evoke a particular line of thought. Like any narrative, they are embellished for effect, by drawing attention to features that overwhelmed or influenced our experience. We see them as creative mixtures of times, scales, and perspectives; yet in no way do they attempt to be definitive or complete.

As anyone who has attempted transcalar thinking can attest, it is difficult and unruly. Coming back to our friend Mr. Palomar, we recall that the character's explorations often end with frustration and exhaustion. These are the side effects of trying to see multiple scales simultaneously within a changing system. Transcalarity is not a recipe to follow; it does not come with a checklist. It requires appreciation, experience, experimentation, patience, and a curiosity about the interdependence of and relationships between things. Once, when Holling was asked for advice about responding to the climate crisis, he wrote, "The only way to approach such a period, in which uncertainty is very large and one cannot predict what the future holds, is not to predict, but to experiment and act inventively and exuberantly via diverse adventures in living."[41] We must celebrate our uncertain futures, and probe them, for embracing the unknown can lead to new transcalar insights. We never know what we might learn by staring at the goose fat, like Mr. Palomar, or walking along the shore of a bay.

5 miles

2

SAGINAW BAY

I N SUMMER THE DRAINAGE DITCH ALONG THE SIDE OF FINN ROAD
is carpeted with bright green duckweed. The small aquatic plant, its
leaves no wider than an eighth of an inch, grows in large mats on the
surface, obscuring the water's depth. The land is incredibly flat, and
there are hundreds of miles of these wide drainage ditches subdividing
the tiled cropland of dry beans, corn, and sugar beets. The ditches
adhere to and shadow the strict grid of this landscape, which serves as
one of the fundamental land-to-water interfaces of the Saginaw Bay.
Most vehicles approach this part of Lake Huron by taking the
highway to Saginaw, following the Saginaw River to Bay City, then
continuing to the river's mouth, which is flanked by a couple of yacht
clubs and the coal dock of a decommissioned power plant. We take a
more idiosyncratic approach, ignoring the mouth of the Saginaw and
instead following the drainage ditches north until the bright green
channels sink into the muted shallows of the lake. At the end of Finn
Road, we park and climb onto a wooden platform perched on a berm.

◀ FIGURE 2.1. Saginaw Bay. Map of the greater Saginaw Bay area, showing general
topography (contours), land use patterns, and urbanized areas (in yellow) in a way
that attempts to limit the clear designation between land and water. Here the pattern
of agricultural fields of the region is clearly evident. Image by the authors.

FIGURE 2.2. Saginaw Bay Field of Phragmites. View of the Saginaw Bay from an overlook at the Quanicassee Wildlife Area. The water's edge is completely obscured by the immense mass of Phragmites. Image by the authors.

While one might expect such a platform to offer a coveted view of the water, we are instead met by a fifteen-foot-high wall made almost entirely of one reed species, *Phragmites australis*. The *Phragmites* field stretches over half a mile, separating the platform from the lake's edge and obscuring any hint of water. *Phragmites* are aggressive, pervasive, and often classified in this region as a nuisance, their dense growth being seen as a threat to shoreline views, species diversity, and public

42

safety. Indeed, their field condition is thick and prominent. They are thriving here, and their agency in this landscape is undeniable and fascinating in its own right. All along this bay, no matter which route one takes, the *Phragmites* will be there, guiding the path to the water's edge. So, in this moment, instead of trying to bypass these reeds, we revel in the condition of the expanded shoreline and allow ourselves to get lost in this thick and shallow edge.

THE CENTER OF IT ALL

The present location of the Saginaw Bay can be understood as a 1,143-square-mile shallow bowl carved along Michigan's Lake Huron shoreline, a result of thousands of years of geologic and hydrologic change (see the interlude by Marcia Bjornerud in this volume). Like much of the Great Lakes region, this shoreland was formed by sedimentation beneath a shallow sea, pushed and pulled by massive glaciers during the Wisconsin Glaciation, then reshaped again by the melting of glacial waters. The current extent of the Saginaw Bay is a geologically momentary blip for a body of water in continuous fluctuation.

Surrounded by water on three sides, Michigan is the self-proclaimed epicenter of all things Great Lakes. This is not just a cultural claim but a geologic one: the land lies in the bullseye of concentric rings of geologic time that the historian William Ashworth compares to a set of "nesting bowls."[1] The Saginaw Bay lies near the center of this formation, on rock beds formed in the Pennsylvanian Epoch, the youngest geologic foundation in the Great Lakes Basin.

Approximately thirteen thousand years ago, the region was covered by one of the first emerging glacial lakes, aptly named Lake Saginaw. The shores of this ancient lake extended deep into present-day Michigan. Our vantage point at the end of Finn Road would have been some fifty miles into that lake. At that point in history, the waters moved in the opposite direction, flowing southwest toward what is now the Mississippi River. As the glaciers retreated, the shoreline of Lake Saginaw (later known as Lake Stanley) moved east into what is today Lake Huron, so that ten thousand years ago our current location would have been almost one hundred miles inland. These fluctuations can be tracked by evidence left within the moving littoral zone, where water and wind push and pull the rocks, sediment, and vegetation into ridges, swales, and slopes. The movement of this active interface indicates where the water has been, and where it may go in the future. But for now, it lies in the wide shallow pan called the Saginaw Bay.

The entire Saginaw region is likewise a shallow gradient of the former lakebed. At many points within the 8,700-square-mile watershed, the river and its floodplain drop only one foot of elevation per linear mile. With such gradual topography, even small changes in water levels can have a large effect on landscape composition. A rise of one inch can cover almost fifty yards, so the water of the bay is constantly giving and taking territory. This is significant within a system where water levels can vary by more than a foot from one year to the next. Of course, water levels rise and fall dramatically in many coastal places, but since ocean tides fluctuate daily, the cycle is better understood by the average observer. The slower cycles of the Great Lakes often allow for several seasons of vegetal growth between high and low conditions, making it appear, to a casual observer or newcomer, that the water levels have permanently changed. The bay's flat, gradual bathymetry, which calms water movement and promotes sediment buildup, has helped establish an edge condition that supports one of the country's largest contiguous freshwater marshes. Covering forty thousand acres of shoreline around the bay, large parts of this marsh are managed by the state of Michigan's Department of Natural Resources (DNR), which is considerably motivated by the hunting and fishing activities that the large coastal environment offers.

PERFORATED AND PLANTED

When the first European colonial settlers arrived in the Saginaw area, the marsh around the bay was likely three times its present size. And while many see the value in wetlands today, in the very recent past they were considered a nuisance. An 1815 report by Surveyor General Edward Tiffin claimed the land was not "worth the cost of surveying," as only "one acre in a hundred was worth cultivation."[2] Yet this sentiment would not last long, for the agricultural potential of this land soon became evident.

At the time of European settlement, central Michigan was a collection of continuous gradients spanning from wetland marshes to upland forests, with extensive pinewoods in the north and hardwoods in the south. Not surprisingly, one of the first settler industries was forestry, and Michigan became a national leader in lumber production. Among a series of other extraction experiments in the mid- to late nineteenth century, the most successful was salt production. Wells dug in central Michigan produced a brine that could be evaporated and processed into salt. This required large amounts of heat, which was supplied by waste wood from the Saginaw Valley lumber mills. Thus, for half a century, the waste of deforestation fueled the production of salt, a process that continued until the old-growth forests were mostly logged and the lumber industry began to decline.[3]

The other significant extracted resource was coal, first discovered in the region in 1861.[4] The Michigan coal industry peaked in 1907, when the state was producing about 2 million short tons through 37 operating mines (still just a minuscule share of the national production of 394 million tons). All these mines were located within the Pennsylvanian Epoch stones of the Saginaw watershed, and most were in Bay and Saginaw Counties. While this coal was lauded for its quality, the costs of production and transport made it more expensive for the Detroit market than coal mined in West Virginia or Ohio. Michigan coal was sent to western markets in Wisconsin, Minnesota, and the Dakotas, but high export costs and low quantity eventually led to the industry's collapse. Today the main reminder of the once-strong industry is the public danger posed by its legacy infrastructure, and there are renewed efforts to locate abandoned coal-mine shafts and fill them to prevent collapse.

Thanks to its unique geology, central Michigan had a bit of everything, but not enough of any one resource to support an extraction economy over the long term. Today the coal, salt, and lumber industries are essentially gone. In the 1950s a significant oil strike in southern Michigan, near the Ohio border, spurred a regional desire to drill exploration wells. As an industry, oil has fared no better than coal or salt, although oil derricks can still be found quietly pumping in agricultural fields. When it came to the extraction industries of the nineteenth and twentieth centuries, Michigan was a jack of all trades and master of

45

none. Yet the short-lived experiments encouraged settlement along the Saginaw River, where the "worthless" marsh landscape Tiffin described was discovered to be extremely fertile ground. By the late 1800s, this once-forested landscape with its rich wetland soils was being drained and planted into the highly productive agricultural region found today.

DITCHED

Now, the roads of central Michigan cut through flat fields providing expansive views of the seasonal choreography of irrigation systems, tractors, backhoes, plows, cultivators, and the like. With more than 45 percent of the land currently used for food production, the Saginaw Bay watershed is an agricultural powerhouse.[5] Unlike in other areas (for example, western Michigan, where existing conditions were ideal for growing fruit trees), farming in central Michigan required significant land alterations, the most notable being the ditches—dense and wide grooves that edge the fields in green networks leading out to the bay.

Ditchdigging in the United States was institutionalized by the federal Swamp Lands Act of 1850, which gave Michigan settlers significant support for the conversion of "swamp or overflow lands unfit for cultivation" into farmland. By 1906 they had "reclaimed" almost as much marshland as settlers in Arkansas, Florida, and Louisiana, for whom the act was originally written.[6] In places like Louisiana, the law was used to fund the creation of embankments and other flood protections to "reclaim" land from the once meandering Mississippi River. Along the Great Lakes, however, draining wetlands was simpler. Farmers merely had to dig ditches and lay drainage tile in order to pull water from the land. Early documentation of this process referenced the Dutch strategy of creating polders as a model for managing wetlands in the Great Lakes Basin, as if this region, too, were battling to save itself from a rising sea.

It is now broadly understood that draining this "undesirable" land has depleted one of the most extensive freshwater wetland ecosystems

◄ FIGURE 2.3. Ditched and Drained. Aerial images of the algae-lined drainage ditches that stretch from the region's agricultural fields to the waters of the Saginaw Bay. Images by the authors.

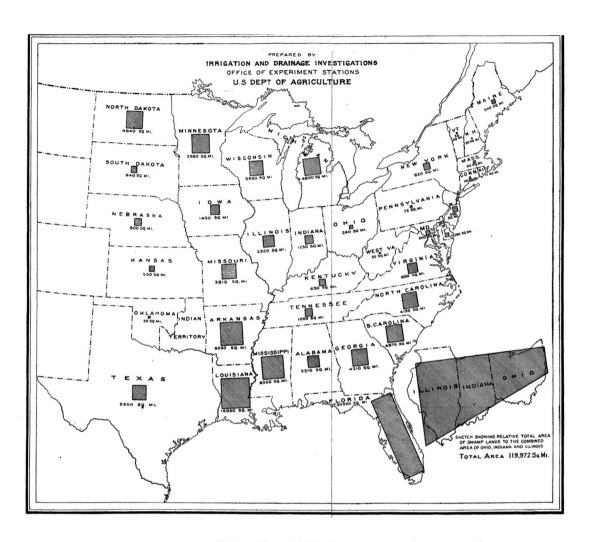

FIGURE 2.4. Unlimited Potential. Map from a 1907 report showing areas of swamp and overflowed lands that were available for reclamation. Notably, large percentages of land are identified in the Great Lakes Region, including Michigan and Wisconsin in particular. Image: United States Department of Agriculture.

in the world. Yet, at the time, the desire to increase arable land out-weighed any other consideration. A map drawn by the US Department of Agriculture's Office of Experiment Stations showed the eastern United States as a mere collection of swamp resources waiting to be "leveraged." The report went so far as to describe the productivity of former wetlands as "unexcelled" in quality, assuming proper flood protection and drainage.[7]

The drainage systems of the Saginaw Bay tracked the patterns of agricultural development determined by the Jeffersonian Grid, so that the land was rendered as a seemingly endless series of quarter-mile crop fields, separated by roads and ditches. This gave rise to a new, small but important Saginaw export industry: the machinery to transform and create such landscapes. The Bay City Dredging Works Company, for example, manufactured a wide range of land-dredging machines, which were used to ditch through wetlands and transform marshes into agricultural land. The most famous of these was a "walking" dredge crane (1916) that eliminated the need for guiding rails.[8] The walking dredge spanned the ditch, its legs spread as wide as thirty feet, and moved slowly forward on patented skid-like feet. Machines manufactured in the Saginaw region were used all over the country, but their signature mark, a wide, deep ditch, is particularly prominent here in the place where they were designed.

With drains pulling the water from the former marshes, Saginaw Bay farmers put the land to productive use, growing apples, potatoes, corn, soybeans, wheat, and more. Today the region is best known for its dry beans and sugar beets. While farmed in a few places within the Midwest, in Saginaw the sugar beet crop and its processing facilities have put these counties on the national stage. The region continues to rank as one of the largest producers of sugar beets in the United States. The sugar beet, a root vegetable that is processed into a sugar product almost interchangeable with that made from sugarcane, does especially well in the soils and climate of this bay region, tolerating the water fluctuations and benefiting from cold temperatures in the fall and winter.

Like other crops, sugar beets are fertilized with nitrogen and phosphates, and the excess runs off fields into the drainage systems, contributing to nutrient pollution in the bay. This agricultural runoff has been identified by the Environmental Protection Agency (EPA) as one of the primary pollution sources in the Saginaw Bay Area of Concern. Another primary source is industrial waste discharges, where we can also look at beets as an agricultural example. Due to their heaviness and bruisability, sugar beets do not travel well and

49

manufacturing plants are thus often located near the fields.[9] In 1974, the EPA identified two sugar production plants, along with General Motors and Dow Chemical, as the four main polluters of the Saginaw River.[10] Waste from the two sugar plants contributed 98 percent of the total industrial BOD (biochemical oxygen demand) in the study year.

PHRAGMITES

The waste in the Saginaw River from agriculture, other industry, and development travels down to the bay where it meets a fairly new emergent monoculture. As we see from the platform at the end of Finn Road, the extensive wetlands along the lake edge are now largely defined by a nonnative variety of *Phragmites*. This condition is a result of the unique characteristics of the plant as well as the particulars of the site. From a vantage point at the Quanicassee Wildlife Area at the supposed shoreline of the bay, there is no clear and decisive point where water meets land. Instead, *Phragmites* occupies a thick gradient that spans from wet to dry, blurring all attempts at clear coastal delineation.

While it has a native cousin, the European variety of *Phragmites* is more aggressive and has spread quickly and abundantly across North America. As a perennial grass with an incredible capacity to spread (through both seed and rhizomes), it adapts to a variety of regions and watery conditions.[11] *Phragmites* regenerates quickly, tolerates both freshwater and saltwater, and can thrive in degraded soils where other plants often fail. It occupies habitat niches where it faces minimal competition in its initial growth phases, and once established it is very hard to eradicate. Preferring wet soil and full sun, and able to thrive on contaminated sites and in fluctuating conditions, the reed does well along shorelines.[12] Along with the shorelines, it is also often seen on disturbed and newly emergent land such as highway edges, construction sites, lowlands, and ditches, typologies that are all abundant in the Saginaw Bay.

◄ FIGURE 2.5. *Phragmites* Time. A series of images capturing the movement of stems, leaves, light, and wind within a *Phragmites* stand over the period of twenty-four hours. Depending on wind and sun conditions, the pulsing of this landscape can vary considerably. Image by the authors.

While the deep drain ditches that striate the fields of the Saginaw Bay have established it as a productive agricultural region, the ditched and planted landscape has also generated a particular type of disturbance regime. As the fields grow acre after acre of planted monocultures, the soils are subjected to draining, dredging, digging, and the deposition of chemicals, waste, and excess nutrients. Few plants flourish in such highly disturbed hydric conditions better than *Phragmites*, as shown by its nearly ubiquitous distribution across the littoral zone.

The *Phragmites* spread was further enabled by a long period of low water levels throughout the Great Lakes from 1998 to 2013, which provided wide expanses of newly emergent land. Once established, extensive rhizomatic roots of *Phragmites* made it incredibly resilient to environmental changes and challenges and helped it survive when the long period of low water conditions was followed by years of record high water. Now, a landscape that once supported a marshland gradient full of species such as bulrush, aster, goldenrod, willow, and cattails has been transformed into its own wild monoculture, mirroring the mass of agricultural fields in the landscapes beyond.

Along this thick marsh edge are several points of access and circulation maintained by the Michigan DNR. As the ditches slice toward the bay from the fields, they meet the boundary of the state lands and are adorned with boat ramps and parking spots. These slim navigation channels provide some of the few options for penetrating the thick wall of *Phragmites* that armors the shore, and so they naturally take the role of access for fishing and waterfowl hunting. That said, the access is variable. Sometimes channel waters are so high that they submerge the docks and at other times they run completely dry, setting the docks down on the dry ground.

Trails running along the marsh connect with other public lands near the shore. Sometimes a trail follows the lipped edge where the

◄ FIGURE 2.6. Scales of Influence. Composite image showing the relationship between the phosphorus- and nitrogen-filled canals and the growth of *Phragmites* along the Saginaw Bay. From the individual stalks of the reed to the huge masses it generates, the experience of the landscape is highly dictated by this one particular plant. Image by the authors.

marsh meets the agriculture fields, forcing a blatant confrontation between two monocultural grass species and illuminating the limits of human control. On the upland side we see vast stretches of field corn, intentionally planted in clean straight rows. A member of the Poaceae (grass) family, most corn grown in this region has been modified and planted to produce the orderly and highly productive organism situated in the striated fields. From its genes (often genetically modified) to its spacing and nutrient intakes, this corn is thoroughly under control. Across the trail, though, the corn gazes head-to-head with its distant rambunctious cousin, *Phragmites*.

If the landscape of corn reflects an extreme of vegetal control, then the *Phragmites* stand epitomizes the vegetal wild. *Phragmites* thrives through its own natural adaptations, having found ways of growing on almost every continent without the direct help of humans.[13] While the cornfields are replanted every year and coaxed along with the help of fertilizer, *Phragmites* survives on its own, despite continuous efforts to eradicate it. As the farm fields leach excess phosphorus and nitrogen, the waterways bring these agricultural amplifiers down to the shore and sink them into a ground thick with *Phragmites* roots and rhizomes. These rhizomes and roots hold a significant portion of the plant's biomass and have been known to extend as deeply underground as the stem does above ground.[14] They create a thickly braided mat that supports the towering stems and bobbing heads through the physical fluctuations of the water's edge. They likewise store energy that allows them to wait out the eradication efforts (burning, mowing, chemical application, etc.) of local land managers. The Quanicassee Wildlife Area serves as a glowing example of this resilience, as host to a series of *Phragmites* management test-plot sites, many of which are still full of *Phragmites*.

As the corn follows tight lines dictated by machines, in neat rows and clear channels, *Phragmites* grow in dense impenetrable clumps. At times the reeds give way to narrow deer paths, but without constant travel these too become quickly overgrown. Descending into

▶ FIGURE 2.7. Tangled Transect. Collection of sequential images showing the shifting density and space experienced as one walks through a stand of *Phragmites* and attempts to remain oriented. Image by the authors.

a *Phragmites* stand offers a lesson in disorientation because it has no order, no openings, just plants—everywhere. Wayfinding is limited to sun position, water depth, and maybe the occasional glimpse of a tree. After hiking for just a few minutes we find ourselves immersed in a deafening rustling and clicking of stems blowing in the wind. It is perhaps one of the closest experiences to being "inside" of another organism that we can imagine. Now we can understand the news stories from around the world that have described people getting lost for days in *Phragmites*. Taking students out in these stands involves strict instructions for partnering and plans for locating each other during fieldwork. On one memorable kayaking trip, a couple of landscape architecture students took turns paddling quickly and launching themselves into the side of the reed stand. Kayak after kayak, the thick wall of *Phragmites* caught the boats like arrows in a hay bale, holding them within its mass.

CEDING CONTROL

While we immerse ourselves in these stands and play with their remarkable boat-holding density, we recognize that this density, this height, this uncontrollable expanse is what has led many land managers and citizen groups across the Great Lakes to spend millions of dollars in trying to control and eradicate this species. They are not alone: across the country the plant is "battled"; it is mowed, burned, and sprayed heavily with chemicals, all in the name of habitat diversity, water access, or human safety. While the dominant approach here is a militaristic "command and control" a longer glance at landscape history sheds light on the influences that attracted the *Phragmites* in the first place, the shoreline sediments full of excess nutrients and legacy contaminants.[15] In the Saginaw Bay, the *Phragmites* are seen as another environmental hazard, but this narrow view overlooks a more interesting relationship. While unpopular with many, an accumulating body of scholarship recognizes the benefits and uses of *Phragmites*, including

56

▶ FIGURE 2.8. Saginaw Matrix. Collection of curated images from visits to the Saginaw Bay region. Images by the authors.

phytoremediation, which could be incredibly helpful on this contaminated shore.[16] This is an old species that has been lived with, even lived in, for thousands of years.[17] In other parts of the world, it has long been heralded for its productivity and its ability to withstand saturation. It is used as a building material for thatching, paper, mats, rafts, baskets, and tools, for land stabilization and erosion control, and more recently for biofuel.[18] Also, research on management of *Phragmites* suggests that living "with" the species, such as grazing animals in it, using it as a material, and so on, may curb its undesirable invasive qualities while providing resources and ecosystem services.[19] All these uses would seem to align well with the local economic interest in productivity around the Great Lakes. However, even as practice and research continue to recognize the inadequacy of "command and control" management of Phragmites, land managers across the basin continue choosing to approach the species with eradication methods that are often toxic and destructive.[20] It is clear that these approaches to Phragmites, like all land management, are strongly tied to the values and ethics of those managing the land.[21] Research done on Anishinaabe approaches to the invasive species of both *Phragmites* and cattails in Michigan by Nicholas Reo, a Sault Ste. Marie Chippewa, likewise recognizes a key distinction between Euro-American land ethics and those of the Anishinaabe tribal members.[22] While observing that all individuals hold their own worldviews, Reo notes that many members approach the work with the Anishinaabe philosophy of "aki" recognizing the importance of relating to all species as kin, not as "separate"; and the responsibility humans have to understand and nurture with all species.[23] Here in the shallows of the Saginaw Bay, where the ditches and the *Phragmites* lead us to the water's edge, we see how they might also lead us to a better relationship with the water, one that cedes "command and control," recognizing the benefits offered in the mass. We accept the invitation to get a bit lost.

INTERLUDE

ECOLOGICAL NOVELTY AND MANAGEMENT OF THE LITTORAL ZONE

Mark Davis

Mark Davis, the DeWitt Wallace Professor of Biology at Macalester College, is an internationally recognized ecologist. He has authored more than fifty articles and book chapters, being the primary author on all but four of the publications. His work has been cited more than five thousand times. During the past ten years, he has focused his research and writing on invasive species. His book on this topic, *Invasion Biology*, was published by Oxford University Press in January 2009. He holds a doctorate in biology from Dartmouth College, an MA in education from Harvard University, and a BA in the history of science from Harvard University.

I N THE PAST FEW YEARS, A NEW PERSPECTIVE HAS BEEN TAKING HOLD in the field of ecology. Referred to as "ecological novelty" it emphasizes that many factors are rapidly producing ecologically novel environments. Climate change (which includes changes in temperatures and patterns of precipitation), increased atmospheric CO_2, which affects photosynthetic rates, increased availability of nitrogen (due to worldwide atmospheric nitrogen deposition and nitrogen runoff into aquatic systems), and the introduction of new species are all rapidly changing our environments and creating new combinations of physical and biological processes and states.

Rapid change often brings with it considerable anxiety since it is not clear where the rapid change will lead. In the early 2000s, the humanist Svetlana Boym wrote a book on how people respond to rapid changes. According to Boym, rapid change commonly elicits strong feelings of nostalgia. In her book, *The Future of Nostalgia*, Boym argued that people tend to adopt one of two types of nostalgia when confronted with rapid change.[1]

The first she called "restorative nostalgia." Restorative nostalgia, Boym said, knows two main plots—the return to origins and the conspiracy that "home" is forever under siege requiring defense against the common enemy. In other words, this is a longing to return to the native state, to the way things used to be. The longing to return to the past is often accompanied by the belief that the rapid change is due to the presence of newcomers who are contributing to the rapid change. Under restorative nostalgia, when confronted by this threat of newcomers, efforts must be undertaken to rid the homeland of the invader, to eradicate them.

Boym described the second type of nostalgia as "reflective nostalgia." Under rapid change, reflective nostalgia recognizes the sense of loss of the past, but it is not hell-bent on restoring the past, nor does it brand the newcomers as the enemy and declare war on them. Rather, reflective nostalgia remembers the past and creatively tries to develop a way forward that integrates aspects of the past with the current changes to create a path to a secure and meaningful future.

For several decades after their founding in the 1980s, restoration ecology and conservation biology mostly proceeded under the restorative nostalgia approach. Restoration ecology emerged as an effort to restore and return habitats back to an earlier state, in particular one that did not include nonnative species. In 1994 the Society of Ecological Restoration declared that ideally, a restoration project should consist entirely of indigenous species. This nativism perspective dominated into the 2000s when the society urged that the control of exotic species should be an integral component of all restoration projects and programs.

Conservation biology also adopted the nativism paradigm in defining conservation goals. In 1990 the conservation biologist Stanley Temple starkly stated in the journal *Conservation Biology*, "Conservation biologists should be as proficient at eradicating exotic species as they are at saving endangered species."[2]

The desire to restore the past and to rid oneself of newcomers is a common human response to very rapid change. The past is reassuring in its familiarity. Rapid change, whether cultural, political, or ecological, threatens the persistence of traditional norms whether they are practices, beliefs, or ecosystems.

MARK DAVIS

The ecological novelty paradigm differs dramatically from more value-based and agenda-driven paradigms of nature. For example, ecological restoration has a specific agenda to assist the recovery of an ecosystem that has been degraded, damaged, or destroyed. A strength of the term "ecological novelty" is that it is only descriptive. It simply states that ecosystems are changing and are different from the way they were in the past, even the recent past. It says nothing about whether this change is good or bad. And it does not indicate a direction toward which ecosystem management should proceed. In other words, under the ecological management program all possible directions are available for ecosystem managers. Management goals are not based on predetermined objectives but are developed depending on what society desires at this point in time with respect to the functions and inhabitants of the ecosystem and on what is going to be ecologically and economically feasible.

These ideas are very relevant to the management of littoral zone environments of the Great Lakes, many of which are changing rapidly in their ecosystem functions and inhabitants due to climate change, eutrophication, and the introduction of novel species. The knee-jerk reaction is to view the changes as damaging and to create a management plan that will try to restore the ecosystem back to a preexisting state. But what is the preexisting state? The Great Lakes have undergone so many physical and biological changes in the past century that it is not clear what the preexisting state is or should be. While some of the changes may be viewed as undesirable, it is possible some of the changes may be viewed as neutral or even desirable. For example, both the Society for Ecological Restoration and the US Fish and Wildlife Service now acknowledge that in some instances it may be in our best interest to incorporate some nonnative species into the management plan, given the desired ecosystem effects of these species.

Adopting the ecological novelty paradigm should be liberating for managers of the littoral zones of the Great Lakes. It is not agenda driven and managers thus have the opportunity and freedom to think about the littoral zone ecosystems in new ways. Management under the ecological paradigm does not ignore the past, but neither is it bound by it. In other words, ecological novelty can be an incentive to think about the management of these ecosystems in novel ways.

63

5 miles

3

NIPIGON BAY

AN OVERLOOK ALONG THE NIPIGON RIVER RECREATION TRAIL affords a sweeping view over the northern reaches of Nipigon Bay. Here the steep geologic bedrock makes up much of the shoreline and provides mountainous views of the water below. Perched high, we can see across most of the bay and up the Nipigon River, which feeds the bay water from Lake Nipigon to the north. The feeling of isolation is quite strong. The northern shore of Lake Superior between Sault Ste. Marie and Thunder Bay may be the least developed stretch of coastline in the entire Great Lakes Basin. Along these 450 miles of the Trans-Canada Highway are only a handful of towns with more than a thousand people. The area appears rugged and quiet, and local interests have leveraged those qualities in their marketing. A sign welcoming us to town reads "Nipigon: A Natural Edge," and indeed our expansive view of steep cliffs and vast tracts of boreal forest corroborates the advertisement. There are few opportunities to venture off

◄ FIGURE 3.1. Nipigon Bay. Map of the greater Nipigon Bay area, showing general topography (contours), land use patterns, and urbanized areas (in yellow) in a way that attempts to limit the clear designation between land and water. The position of the bay as a transition between the landscape to the north and Lake Superior can be observed here; in addition, the image reveals the Nipigon Bay as one of several bays tucked into this shoreline. Image by the authors.

the highway, and they always seem to terminate in a dead end or a body of water. Directly below the overlook is the small town of Red Rock, purportedly the continent's northernmost freshwater port (when it is not frozen over). During much of the year, the ground is blanketed in snow; daytime temperatures in January range between twelve degrees and minus eleven degrees Fahrenheit. Traveling in summer, we evade those frigid temperatures, but their influence is visible everywhere. In Beardmore, a former gold-mining town between Lake Nipigon and Nipigon Bay, greetings come by way of a permanent thirty-five-foot-tall snowman holding a fishing rod. Supposedly the rod is replaced with a curling broom in the winter, but regardless of season, it seems fitting that there is always a snowman at the edge of this northern town.

A BLANKET OF WIRES

From our spot above Red Rock, the clarity of this particular morning allows for an easy count of several rocky humps on the surface of the bay, the largest of which is known as Vert Island. We play with and emphasize these shifts in a collage of photographs taken over the course of twenty-four hours from the shoreline below. Vert Island might seem to be just another rocky outcropping, floating in and out of the fog of the bay, but it has a history that sets it apart from the others. Mined for sandstone during one of the most significant periods of urbanization in Great Lakes history, the island's rock was used in the reconstruction of Chicago after the fire of 1871. Two decades later, work at the quarry was mostly abandoned due to numerous shipwrecks along the dangerous route between Nipigon Bay and Chicago.[1] Yet, over its short period of operation, the sandstone was used in many buildings by prominent Chicago architects, including Adler and Sullivan and Burnham and Root.[2] Most of those buildings have since been demolished, but a preserved corner of William Le Baron Jenney's Home Insurance Building can still be found at the Chicago Museum of Science and Industry. Famous for being the first skyscraper with a structural steel frame, the building was also clad with sandstone from Vert Island. This design detail brought part of Vert Island, located in one of the most remote corners of the basin, into the heart of the region's largest metropolis and incorporated its material into a design

FIGURE 3.2. Visions of Vert Island. Time-lapse images of Vert Island in the Nipigon Bay over the course of twenty-four hours. While from this vantage it is partially obscured by the smaller La Grange Island in the foreground, the presence of Vert Island and the impact it has had across the region can be both felt and seen if you look for it. Image by the authors.

advancement that would change the skyline of cities throughout the world. This history, having now extended beyond living human memory and being followed by over a century of minimal activity on this remote island, is now relegated on both ends (source and destination) to museums, written records, and the occasional tag on a map.

67

Mining sites, both past and present, pepper the landscape, but the extractive industry that most clearly defines Nipigon today is hydroelectric power with its large network of roads, wires, and dams overrunning the landscape. Enormous clear-cuts push back the forest from towering electrical wires, and the Trans-Canada Highway runs through deep corridors of blasted rock. As it turns out, our drive coincides with a highway-widening project, which means frequent stops watching road workers swing their stop signs back and forth as rock formations created over millions of years, moved and compacted by glaciers, are blasted away to make room for automobiles. Cleared to continue, we pass chunks lying alongside the road, waiting to be ground down by machines and transported elsewhere, at a decidedly nonglacial pace.

Many roads around the Great Lakes closely follow the shoreline at lake level, but here the highway serves long-distance travelers and is held away from the water. The route gently climbs and descends through ancient geological layers, offering dramatic views of the lake at highway pull offs. Power lines are everywhere: parting the tree line, bridging the highway, sometimes merging alongside it to collectively slice through the landscape. This organization is particularly evident as the drive continues west past Nipigon toward Thunder Bay. Here the landscape implications of the hydroelectric dams on the Nipigon River can be seen most clearly. Canada is the world's fourth largest producer of hydropower.[3] The three stations along the Nipigon River collectively generate over three hundred megawatts of power.[4] This seemingly quiet corner of Ontario is centrally located in an intricate web of generation stations and transmission corridors that keep the vast territory of Canada electrified.

When we check in early at a highway hotel west of town, the desk clerk notes that we are lucky to get a room, as they are almost sold out. Looking out on the abandoned parking lot and recalling the solitary drive, we are initially puzzled by this remark, but, eager to continue our explorations, we quickly drop off a few things and do not think much of it. We continue our drive north along the river toward enormous Lake Nipigon, which sits 250 feet above Lake Superior and is considered by many to be the headwaters of the entire Great Lakes system.[5] The river that spans this drop was historically a fish-filled collection of wild rapids and small lakes until the waterway was harnessed for hydroelectricity in the first half of the twentieth century.[6] The Nipigon River is the largest contributor of water to Lake Superior, but now the water arrives as the by-product of a hydroelectric machine that has completely transformed the region's ecology.

Over the course of a generation, four dams were constructed here, altering the water levels and the shorelines of the river and its lakes. When the Virgin Falls Dam was completed in 1925, it transformed Lake Nipigon into the world's largest water-storage reservoir. But that record would not stand for long. Pine Portage Dam, built in 1950, raised Lake Nipigon by almost five inches, elevating water levels in the river by one hundred feet, an act that completely submerged the rapids, waterfalls, lakes, and the Virgin Falls Dam itself.[7] The impounded Lake Nipigon, which now covers 1,800 square miles, is almost two feet higher than it was before the dams were constructed.

The Pine Portage generating station is at the literal end of the road as we head north along the river through rocky, wooded terrain. The drive is characterized by the now familiar collection of overhead wires and a steady flow of large white pickup trucks with energy company logos on their sides. Our rented black SUV with Minnesota plates draws stares—reminding us of a colleague's advice that the best way to explore rural areas without harassment is to get a white pickup truck and act like you know what you are doing—but none of the hydro-company personnel stop to question us.

The public-access road rises up and stops at the edge of Pine Portage Dam, where there is a small lookout over the flooded territory, now effectively an extension of Lake Nipigon's South Bay. Atop this giant berm created by the dam's construction, we survey a crumbling, stone boat dock and a rich mix of weedy wildflowers at the river's edge. We can hear the water rushing below us. Signs warn about infrastructural dangers such as strong currents and shocks, as we scramble around on the rocks that reinforce the bank. For such a transformative intervention, the decades of growth have seemingly tucked Pine Portage back into the landscape, making it difficult to imagine the wild river that would have once been here.

On the way back to town, we search for the other two remaining dams. From a designated viewing area at Alexander Falls, we hike

69

FIGURE 3.3. The Blanket of Wires. Composite image exploring the impact of various experiences of the Nipigon region. Here, the trucks from hydroelectric companies seem to be stretching wires across the region, stitching together what first appeared as a quiet landscape blanketed in lichen. Image by the authors.

down to see the generating station at eye level and the exposed stone substrate of the river's edge. Here the old log flume that was used to drive logs around the dam is visible and identified through a pair of interpretive signs. As the day wanes, the mosquitoes multiply, discouraging us from lingering. Back at the hotel, we finally understand the comment from the receptionist: the parking lot is stacked with those white pickup trucks.

As the trucks attest, the dams and power-transmission corridors here are the most prominent nodes of mediation between the landscape and human interests. The networked infrastructure connects the bay not only to the urban regions east and west but also to remote areas farther north. In 1943 an engineering project known as the Ogoki diversion redirected an entire watershed toward Lake Nipigon and increased the flow into Lake Superior by 50 percent, boosting hydroelectric potential not just along the Nipigon River but at generating stations from Sault Ste. Marie to Niagara, hundreds of miles away.[8] Everything here is unapologetically linked into a landscape machine for energy production. What felt like open wilderness when we first arrived at the "Natural Edge" of Nipigon now seems imprisoned by wires and regulated water levels.

AN AFTERNOON AT THE MUSEUM

> The Nipigon River has always been famous for three things; its beauty, its trout and the fact that it was considered undrivable.
>
> —John Kelso and James Demers, *Our Living Heritage*

One rainy afternoon, we stumble into the Nipigon Museum for a chance to dry off. While not large, the museum is packed with memorabilia and local history passed along by families and businesses through the centuries. Once upon a time, the main attraction was the world-record brook trout caught by Dr. J. W. Cook in 1915, which brought national fame to Nipigon—a 14.5-pound fish landed on a simple fly-fishing tackle. The museum still has the original rod and reel on display, although the fish itself, skinned and mounted on birch bark, was damaged in a fire in 1990. The museum now hosts its charred remains alongside a collection of replicas. Accompanying a robust assortment of fish-themed exhibition items is a growing collection of donated scrapbooks, photos, and artifacts that show the close relation between the settlers who have lived here, the river, and the power it has provided.

Before (and after) the dams were constructed, the river was used for transporting timber. Spruce and pine trees were logged first for the advancing railroad, and then for the production of poles and cut lumber. Today many of these trees end up as pulpwood. As found elsewhere in the basin, logging operations dramatically altered the landscape through clear-cutting, monoculture plantings, and other methods of forestry management that contribute to habitat loss and fragmentation. By 1990, almost every woodland had been harvested at least once, with the exception of some islands in Lake Nipigon.[9] Cut logs were "driven" down the Nipigon River toward Lake Helen, where they were bound and shipped elsewhere. Historic images show large expanses of southern Lake Nipigon, north of the Virgin Falls Dam, covered with logs, ready to be spilled downriver. Drive crews armed with alligator boats and pike poles helped move the logs, breaking up jams along the way.[10] Later, the rafts of logs had to be diverted around the dams in log chutes like the one we saw at the Alexander facility.

While the dams were erasing rapids and flooding valleys, the floating timber was depositing large amounts of bark and other woody debris onto the lake and riverbeds. Both of these modifications contributed to the decline of the highly valued fishing industry and eventually led to the river's listing as an Area of Concern. Early land managers foresaw these problems, but their conservation efforts were intermittent. In 1911 log drives were prohibited in Ontario due to concerns about their impact on fisheries, but the ban was lifted only twelve years later.[11] Similarly, the Lake Nipigon Provincial Forest temporarily protected trees around the lake, until it was disbanded several decades later during a strong timber market.[12] More recent efforts to limit the effects of logging and mineral extraction have been channeled through the designation of the Lake Nipigon Basin

▶ FIGURE 3.4. Historic Nipigon. Above: 1930s image of men driving logs over Alexander Falls Generation Station on the Nipigon River. Below: Postcard, sold by the Canadian Postcard Company in 1939, advertising the amazing fishing to be found in Nipigon. Images: Thunder Bay Museum.

LOADING OUR CATCH

COPYRIGHT CANADA 1936 BY
CANADIAN POST CARD CO., TORONTO

At Nipigon, Ontario

Signature Site, but it is not yet clear whether these regulations, too, will be weakened in the face of growing industrial demand.

On one wall of the small museum, we find a large Hudson Bay Company sign. The attendant tells us it was "saved from the trash" when the iconic company, which maintained an outpost in Nipigon for hundreds of years, finally closed in 1972. As the British trade and import dealer for the vast majority of central Canada, the company coordinated the lives of many early settlers. Its influence in Nipigon is evident in the piles of scrapbooks documenting clubs, parties, and other events hosted at or by the company. As do so many museums, historical societies, and clubs in the small towns within the basin, this collection depicts a rich history and plays a critical role in sharing stories of this place. But, again like so many others, it is almost exclusively focused on a colonial history.

When such museums have an Indigenous or First Nations section, it is typically a single corner that depicts a story of the past through artifacts such as arrowheads, baskets, and jewelry. In these corners, there is little or no mention of the mass trauma and injustices that have been and continue to be perpetrated upon Indigenous and First Nation people throughout the Great Lakes. Communities including the Cree, Dakota, Sioux, and Ojibwe have lived in the Nipigon watershed for thousands of years.[13] Long before white pickup trucks arrived or any newsworthy trout were caught, the First Nations fished and followed the hunt of woodland caribou through the thick boreal forest.[14] From the time of the first colonial explorers to the series of treaties made with European settlers beginning in the 1700s, their rights and relationship to the land have been marginalized and threatened. In this region, the Robinson-Superior Treaty of 1850 "officiated" the colonial taking of the land through a onetime payment of £2,000 and a per annum payment of £500 to the tribes, with stipulations that the First Nation peoples would retain hunting and fishing rights until the land was developed and that they would

▶ FIGURE 3.5. Looking at Lichen. Composite image describing the experiential qualities of lichen and the unique landscape of the Nipigon Bay. Backdrops of misty forests and rock outcroppings are bespeckled by this slow-growing contextual microcosm. Image by the authors.

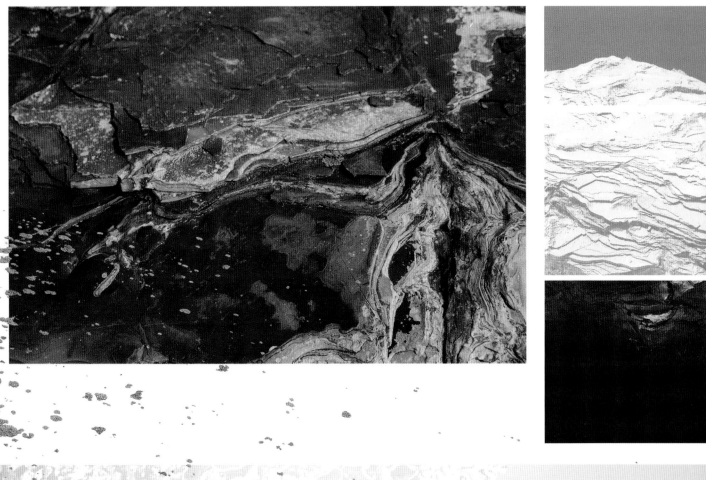

receive rights to their own land in the form of "reserves."[15] As noted by the Anishinabek Nation's account, the First Nations had long shared governance amongst themselves through the use of treaties, and they were following suit in negotiating with the Europeans.[16] But by all evidence and accounts, these treaties did not and do not do justice for the First Nations. Additionally, governmental movements in both Canada and the United States aimed to weaken Indigenous cultural legacies and practices through actions such as the widespread removal of Indigenous children from their homes, their imprisonment in boarding schools under harsh conditions, or their placement for adoption in white families. The effects of these programs have been and continue to be incredibly harmful and traumatic to both individuals and communities.

Unlike some other regions of the Great Lakes, such as Maumee Bay, where Indigenous people were almost completely driven out, First Nation communities continue to live in the Nipigon/Red Rock area.[17] The professor Patricia D. Maguire, an Anishinaabe Wiisaakodewikwe affiliated with Bingwi Neyaashi Anishinaabe, has shared stories of this region passed down from her family in some of her writings and her doctoral dissertation. She writes: "Anishinaabe Diabaajimtow Nadagikenim—stories are the mainstay of Anishinaabe knowledges. They speak to us of our life. Stories told me how to deal with the world, how to learn and how to behave. Stories told me who I was, where my territory was, and who my people were."[18]

The stories, collected orally, rarely dwell on dates and official records, but rather fold events such as treaty signings into lessons of character, values, traditions, and relationships between people and the land. Such an approach recognizes the role of the storyteller, not in a passive position, but involved in an active practice taking responsibility for the past, but also the present and the future.

AN ANCIENT MICROCOSM

Even at the height of the summer tourist season, exploring the forests and shorelines around Nipigon Bay—clambering across rocks and hiking past dense patches of bright purple lupine—is a solitary experience. The geology is strikingly different here than it is along other Great

Lakes shorelines, as rocky beaches and large bedrock outcroppings plunge into the clear, near-freezing water. Any curiosity about why more people do not live in this picturesque landscape would likely be answered by a visit in winter, when ice and snow covers the shores from at least September to May. With frigid temperatures and deep snowfall, vegetation growth is subdued, and the plants and animals must be highly adapted to live in extreme conditions. Among the resilient organisms that have thrived in this harsh environment are the lichens. While easy to overlook, a close study of the surfaces of rocks and trees reveals a landscape thick with an incredible variety of colors, forms, and distributions.

On the Nipigon River Recreation Trail, views across the bay are tempered by the captivating world beneath our feet. Defended by prodigious amounts of insect repellent, we ramble along the trail, lifting logs, feeling trunks, and collecting photographs and samples of different lichen. In Nipigon country, they grow everywhere from trash cans and buildings to the trunks of majestic pine trees, but one of our favorite collections appears on the massive boulders of the rocky Lake Superior shorelines. Traversing these large stones, our fingers and occasionally our cheeks press against the rocks, and we can feel their warmth and capacity to hold the sun's heat even after a fog has settled in. These massive half-submerged boulders are microenvironments of fantastic order. We trace the lines of minerals that reveal ancient geologic shifts, crouch down to test the temperature of a small pool of water and feel the petals of a small flower growing in a thin crevice. Mostly, though, we run our fingers across the mottled softness of the lichen colonies that spread in bursts of bright yellow, orange, and white across the surfaces of stone and peer at them through small magnifying lenses. Once tuned into their forms and expressions, it is hard not to be lured by the lichens, and we seek them out at every turn.

Lichens have been studied for centuries, but science is now reassessing what is really known about these organisms. Questions as fundamental as when lichens first evolved and whether they preceded plants are still being debated.[19] Most recent accounts say they have been around for at least 250 million years.[20] They include around 28,000 named species, varying in their habitat, substrate, form, color, and makeup.[21] They are estimated to cover about 7 percent of the terrestrial surface, with varieties that grow on almost every type of substrate. Some even grow inside of rocks, while others never attach to anything at all and are merely carried by the wind.[22]

While the variation is incredible, what these species have in common is that they are often recognized as a single organism while actually comprising at least two or sometimes three different species together in a symbiotic relationship. Most often this relationship includes at least one fungus and at least one photobiont, such as green algae or Cyanobacteria, which perform photosynthesis. The defining characteristic of a lichen is that it is never a single entity, but rather a microcosm, an outcome of these organisms working together to form something else, which would not exist without their relationship. Some biologists consider lichen both an organism and an ecosystem.[23]

In extremely cold environments such as Nipigon Bay, where the variety and mass of vegetation is limited, lichens provide critical food and habitat for numerous species, thanks to their ability to fix airborne nitrogen and make it available as a nutrient. Lichens are also known as bioindicators of environmental health. Since they receive most of their nutrients directly from air and water, shifts in environmental particulates elicit fairly swift responses. While certain species of lichens can be sensitive to change and pollutants, there are also other species of lichen that are able to thrive in incredibly toxic places and live in some of the harshest, most extreme environments. They can withstand major shifts in temperature, light, nutrients, water, and pressure. In several studies certain types of lichens have even been released into outer space and subjected to environments analogous to those of Mars without significant effect.[24]

In Nipigon, lichen provide a critical winter food source for woodland caribou (*Rangifer tarandus caribou*), which move snow with their hooves to find and eat reindeer lichen growing on the forest floor. The

▶ FIGURE 3.6. Lake Nipigon and Nipigon Bay. Top image: Nipigon Bay is the outlet, via the Nipigon River, of Lake Nipigon. While quite remote and unpopulated, several small public landscapes do exist on the lake, such as the Poplar Lodge Park shown here. Bottom image: If you can locate ways across the rail and power infrastructure, you will find that the northern shores of the Nipigon Bay are lined with isolated rocky beaches. Image by the authors.

caribou also graze on other lichens such as oakmoss (*Evernia* spp.), horsehair lichen (*Bryoria* spp.), and beard lichen (*Usnea* spp.). As of 2012, roughly five thousand forest-dwelling woodland caribou were in northern Ontario, but their habitat is moving and shrinking due to factors like climate change, mining, and logging.[25] Now listed as a threatened species, woodland caribou are projected to lose most of their habitat by the end of the century, putting them at risk of extinction.[26] Unfortunately, we have not seen any caribou during our time in Nipigon Bay, nor all that many people. Yet their absence is happily filled by our new fascination with the microcosmic connections happening all around us.

BECOMING LICHEN

On one of the sunnier afternoons, we take a moment and lie down on one of those lichen-covered boulders. Our legs bend along the curve of the rock and we close our eyes. Anyone passing along the trail might think we have just fallen asleep, and it would not be far from true, but at this moment, on that rock, we are not asleep, just busy trying to be lichen. While it may be a bit silly, it is definitely comfortable and might even bring us closer to understanding an organism defined primarily by its symbiotic relationships with others. We have borrowed this activity from Natasha Myers, a professor of anthropology and director of the Plant Studies Collaboratory, who suggests "vegetal-is(ing) your sensorium" as a method to learn more about plants (and lichens!).[27] As humans we will never truly know what it feels like to be decentralized, or in the case of lichens, to become new species through our relationships. Even if our bodies and identities are composed of countless other organisms and are a product of our relations with them, we seldom consider ourselves anything beyond a singular being. For these reasons, it could not hurt to disrupt our typical practices for a moment as we try to get closer to understanding what a lichen world, or as Myers calls it the "Planthropocene," might feel like, or how it might teach us to live differently with each other and with

▶ FIGURE 3.7. Nipigon Bay Matrix. Collection of curated images from visits to the Nipigon Bay region. Images by the authors.

other species. Myers, who has been researching and working on the relationships between people and plants, has made an inspiring call for people to move away from the Anthropocene toward a new era of living that better situates, values, and respects our human relationships with plants and other species. While many plants might fit the bill, we think lichens could be particularly strong teachers in this regard. As the artist Laurie Palmer has so eloquently written in "The Lichen Museum," these organisms provide an immediate challenge to Western classification and capitalist intentions. She writes:

> It is hard to write about lichen because the grammar always seems wrong. As a symbiotic organism, half fungus and half alga, it/they are/is neither singular nor plural, and neither wholly plant (algae are plants) nor fungus (fungi make up their own kingdom). Our seeming incapacity as humans to deal with collective identities has resulted in lichens being classified solely under fungi, "lichenized fungi" to be exact, as if the process of "lichenization" was a kind of paralysis, or colonization enacted by one party on another; as if any two-ness has to involve a hierarchy with one party dominating the other. In contrast, the lichen symbiosis tends to be mutually beneficial in most species. With one foot in each of two taxonomic realms, lichen—tiny, stepped on, slow to grow—rattle the foundations of Western ontology. On top of that, they are anticapitalist. Lichen are anticapitalist because you can't translate their vegetal being or their vital forces into money. Lichen successfully resist human manipulation and exploitation, mainly because they are small and slow, but also because they are a coalition.[28]

Lichens not only survive, but thrive by way of a mutualistic becoming, both within themselves and with their larger context. As the environmental researcher Jennifer Gabrys writes in "Sensing Lichen," "Lichens tune our attention to the relational qualities of organisms."[29] We likewise find that lichens tune our attention to the relational qualities of landscapes. They urge us to ask what we bring to this multispecies exchange and how our relationship with land might go beyond "program," "profession," or "hobby," and instead become inseparable from our own identities.

INTERLUDE

CULTURAL NARRATIVES OF LAKE SUPERIOR'S NORTH SHORE

Mae Davenport

Mae Davenport is a professor in the Department of Forest Resources at the University of Minnesota (UMN) and director of the UMN Center for Changing Landscapes. Her research interests are focused on the human dimensions of natural resource management, specifically sustainable land use planning; community-based ecosystem management; recreation planning and human beliefs, attitudes, and behaviors associated with landscape change. She holds a doctorate in natural resources science and management from the University of Minnesota, an MS in forestry from the University of Montana, Missoula, and a BA in biology and English language and literature from the College of St. Scholastica.

MY WORK IN THE GREAT LAKES BASIN EXPLORES, THROUGH social science research, the contemporary relationships people have with the basin's ever-changing natural systems. I focus on a 150-mile stretch of Lake Superior's North Shore, within present-day Minnesota. The North Shore's coastal ecosystems are wide-ranging, from upland aspen-birch forests and lowland conifer forests and peatlands to cool-water, volcanic bedrock trout streams and the twelve-thousand-acre estuarine wetlands complex of the Saint Louis River. This portion of the North Shore extends across a multilayered geopolitical landscape. These are Indigenous lands. Three Lake Superior Chippewa Bands have reserved lands along the North Shore and retain treaty rights to hunt, fish, and gather throughout the 1854 Ceded Territory. The North Shore also intersects three Minnesota counties and several coastal communities including the Duluth-Superior metropolitan area, a major Great Lakes port.

In many ways the social system is the most dynamic landscape system of the Lake Superior Basin. Humans for millennia have shaped its hydrologic, geochemical, and biophysical structure and functioning. Before European settlement, Indigenous peoples and communities depended on and adapted to the natural rhythms, cycles, and events of Gichigami, or Lake Superior. Since the arrival of Europeans, the heavy hands of fur traders, loggers, miners, commercial fishers, railroad barons, developers, and tourists—and continued policies and practices of colonization—have hastened and amplified change.

Yet, what continues to draw people in growing numbers to Lake Superior today are the natural rhythms, cycles, and events of its coastal, littoral zone. A growing body of biophysical research investigates how a changing climate will affect Lake Superior and its coasts. These studies model historic climate trends, project future climate scenarios, and estimate the impacts of climate change on forests, fishes, wildlife, and water. In contrast, my sociological research asks: How have and how will human communities adapt to change on the North Shore? Since I first started asking these questions more than a decade ago, my scientific worldview and practice have evolved considerably.

To answer the human adaptation question, I explore the multiple cultural meanings and values the North Shore holds for community members, diversely defined. Cultural narratives of places and place-relationships are critical to effective, efficient, and just environmental policy.[1]

On the North Shore, I observe how place values and meanings shape perceptions, beliefs, and, ultimately, people's physical and social interactions with natural systems. In close collaboration with community partners, I have conducted surveys, interviews, and focus groups with community members, including state, federal, and tribal resource managers, local business owners, local government officials, residents, and visitors. I ask: How has the North Shore changed over time? How has change affected you and your relationship with the North Shore? What can you and North Shore communities do to prepare for change? Through a collaborative process of questioning, listening, sharing, and reflecting on multiple experiences of change on the North Shore, deeper place narratives are revealed, and new narratives can be coproduced.

For example, a series of in-depth interviews ($n = 52$) with natural

86

resource professionals, local business owners, community-based organization representatives, emergency response personnel, and local officials revealed a range of perceptions around climate-related changes on the North Shore.[2] Though some described the region as resistant to climate change, most expressed concern about local impacts they have already observed such as extreme weather, a decline of paper birch and moose, and an increase in wildfires. These findings were further confirmed in a mail survey of residents in the two northern North Shore counties (n = 294) and onsite surveys of summer and winter visitors (n = 2,250).[3] More than 75 percent of visitors and 80 percent of residents surveyed believed that climate change is happening. The vast majority of residents (86 percent) reported noticing changing weather patterns over time. Most residents and visitors expressed high levels of concern about native fish and wildlife species and health of the forest ecosystem. More than half of residents surveyed feel personally responsible to support climate adaptation policies and believe their communities need to do more to prepare. Yet only about one-third believe they have the information they need to make decisions.

Interviews with local leaders exposed four dominant narratives of climate action that can be labeled: (1) apathetic optimism, (2) powerless pessimism, (3) overwhelmed and uncertain, and (4) visionary. Many interviewees expressed feelings of uncertainty and powerlessness. One participant lamented, "I pessimistically think that committees will be formed, plans will be made, and binders will be filled . . . and nothing will be acted on as a community. I think individual businesses, driven by the bottom line, will make some effort to change with the climate, but that we lack the political will to do anything either to prevent or respond to [climate change] as a community."

Most participants had more questions than answers when asked about adapting to change "How do we keep [the region] the way that we want to have it for our communities and for future generations? . . . How do we manage resources like this and how do we protect them, restore them, and prepare them for changes like climate change?" Visionaries described needing transformative change in the way communities understand and prepare for change: "We are already looking at how we might need to begin managing our forest resources differently. We are losing black ash, our hardwood wetland tree species." Another participant observed, "Our heritage and our culture is slipping away, but we have an opportunity to build and grow a new one."

Indigenous communities and tribal and intertribal natural resource management agencies have been visionaries and pragmatic leaders in climate adaptation work throughout the region, conducting climate adaptation planning that draws on thousands of years of "observation, deliberation, recognition and adaptation."[4] This work has identified beings (species) of concern and guidance for stewardship and adaptation across the Great Lakes Basin.[5] The opportunities to learn from traditional knowledges, practices, and teachings of the highly adaptive Indigenous communities in the Great Lakes Basin seem endless.

My own understanding of human-nature relationships and change in the Lake Superior Basin continues to grow. Since 2017 I have been a member of an interdisciplinary and collaborative research partnership with tribes and intertribal organizations in the Lake Superior Basin, aimed at protecting manoomin (wild rice, *Zizania* spp.) and honoring tribal sovereignty. To the Ojibwe, manoomin is a gift from the Creator. Manoomin is central to the Ojibwe migration from the North Atlantic Coast to the Great Lakes Basin more than a thousand years ago. Manoomin continues to be life-giving for tribal members today and remains essential to their physical, spiritual, and cultural health and identity.[6] The range of natural manoomin has been greatly diminished by land use change, altered hydrology, pollution, climate change, and a long legacy of culturally oppressive policies. The project team continues to work together with tribal nations in the Lake Superior Basin to understand the complex interactions within manoomin ecosystems, as well as how to challenge existing power structures and oppressive practices of Western science and management. One of the most important facets of this partnership has been the development of a model for responsible and respectful research between the university and tribes.[7]

To date, natural resources and climate science planning and policy in the Great Lakes Basin and across the United States have been dominated by the narratives of Western science and centralized governance. My research in the Great Lakes Basin aims to support a more culturally transparent and inclusive dialogue about change and to promote environmental policies and actions that are culturally relevant, community scaled, and equitable.

MAE DAVENPORT

5 miles

4

GREEN BAY

LIKE SO MANY OTHER LOCATIONS ACROSS THE BASIN, MUCH
of the Green Bay shoreline is private land, offering very little
public access. What little access there is comes in the form of
unassuming parcels or cookie-cutter municipal parks used by local
communities. Sprinkled along the residential roads serving waterfront properties, these smaller sites are of particular interest as they
tend to provide unique glimpses into local ideals of waterfront
access. Stumbling across one such park, we observe residents using
the grassy lawn—mowed all the way to the water—as a launching
area for both kayaking and windsurfing. While accessible, the
lawn-dominated shoreline shows considerable signs of erosion.
Its tightly mowed surface, exposed to the high water from a recent
storm, is laced with *Typha* stalks deposited in intricate wrack
lines by water surge. The stalks, twisted and overlaid, leave behind
a story of forces of wind and water pulling and pushing one shoreline condition into another. Studying the ground, taking photos

◄ FIGURE 4.1. Green Bay. Map of the greater Green Bay area, showing general
topography (contours), land use patterns, and urbanized areas (in yellow) in a way
that attempts to limit the clear designation between land and water. The long,
isolated form of the bay can easily be discerned. Image by the authors.

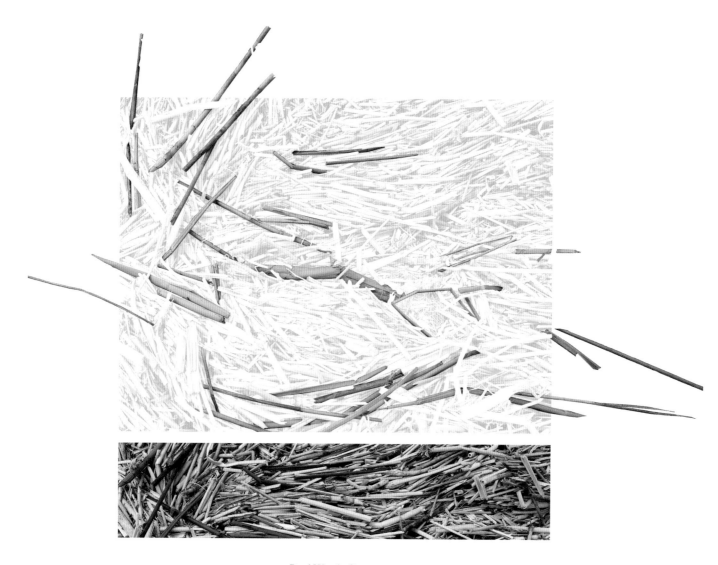

FIGURE 4.2. Reed Wrack. Composite image exploring the pattern and arrangement of individual stems washed onto the shore and collected in a large wrack line. Here the various movements, pulses, and idiosyncrasies of each stalk can be observed and compared either as individual or as part of a larger grouping. Image by the authors.

and sketching, we record these force trajectories as a windsurfer glides along, in a way also tracing the winds across the waters of the bay.

Long and thin, the Green Bay stretches eighty miles northeast from the mouth of the Fox River and the city of Green Bay to the open waters of Lake Michigan. This isolation has fostered the warm, still conditions needed for algae growth, which gives the bay its distinctive color and colonial name. Nearly an isolated lake, the bay is separated from Lake Michigan by a knife-shaped piece of land, the Door Peninsula. This rocky peninsula sits on one end of the Niagara Escarpment, which arcs along the edge of the Michigan Basin, across Lake Huron, and forms Niagara Falls between Lakes Erie and Ontario at its other end. The southwestern part of this rock formation, where present-day Green Bay is located, was carved and smoothed twenty thousand years ago by the extension of the Green Bay lobe of the Wisconsin glaciation. This shift created the significant elevation change that made the Fox River a highly desirable location for industries that could benefit from the moving water.

As is the case elsewhere, much of Green Bay's geologic past has been buried, leveled, settled, or otherwise reconfigured through glacial activity, yet there are still sites where this history can be seen. The Ice Age Trail, a national scenic trail, begins halfway up the Door Peninsula and extends down the bay and across the state, tracing the southern extent of the glaciers. The peninsula is also home to one of the more geologically intrusive infrastructural interventions, the Sturgeon Bay ship canal. The canal cuts through the peninsula, providing a route from Green Bay to Lake Michigan that avoids the hazards of "death's door," the rocky islands at the northern reaches of the bay. It also accommodates a walking trail and nature preserve that make visiting this extreme incision not just a revelatory event but an inviting one. The design of the site is understated, with few indications of its standing as a public place, except for an occasional signboard and a well-worn footpath pointing to the east along the southern edge of the canal. From here, there are long views down to the water where the glacially compressed layers of rock can be seen.

The rock exposed at the Sturgeon Bay ship canal remains because it was strong enough to survive the persistent grinding of the glaciers. Formations that were not as stable were pulverized and spread southward across the landscape by the advancing ice, and those tiny bits of rock are today blended into farm fields, buried under sidewalks, and heaped into the terminal moraines that mark the route of the Ice Age Trail. As they are eroded and washed through the landscape, they will eventually make their way back toward the bay. When they reach slow water, these bits accumulate on the lake bottom and contribute to the bay's shallowing. One of the primary actors in this process is the main tributary feeding the bay, the Fox River.

A RIVER OF PAPER

The Fox River cuts north through the city of Green Bay after draining much of northern Wisconsin. The city itself is rather small, at around 100,000 residents, and has advanced through the typical stages of a Great Lakes port: extraction, prosperity, environmental degradation, and now remediation and reconsideration. The paper industry, which began in the late nineteenth century, was the most formative economic driver, and along the river, large buildings still bear names found in office supply stores. These days they tend to blend in with other industrial structures, making it hard to imagine the scene Dorothy Heesakker described in her 1965 thesis on the Green Bay paper industry as "the lower Fox, so full of power, becoming a river of paper."[1]

It is also hard to see anything powerful about the slow, muddy river as it passes through the city. But in fact the Fox River drops more than 160 vertical feet over 40 miles (an elevation change comparable to Niagara Falls), producing tremendous kinetic energy. The paper mills used the river's water both for generating power and for washing rags, which was originally the first step in paper production. "Washed" is something of a misnomer, as the process involved bleaching rags in a chemical cocktail before they were shredded and pressed, and the effluent passed back to the river. Later, the production and recycling of noncarbon copy paper would add more pollutants, including polychlorinated biphenyls (PCBs), mercury, and ammonia. The paper industry made Green Bay an industrial powerhouse, but in the process it seriously degraded the ecological health of the Fox River watershed. These contaminants are largely why Green Bay was designated an

94

FIGURE 4.3. Aerial View of Green Bay. View looking east toward downtown Green Bay. The Bayport facility is in the foreground and Renard Island is on the upper left in the distance. Image by the authors.

Area of Concern, and they motivate ongoing efforts to improve the region's environmental health.

As we walk along the Fox River Trail one morning, we are able to see some of this remediative work in action. We watch as an excavator

95

picks at a barge piled with sand and places the material on the river bottom. This sand will cap the contaminated mud on the river floor, fixing it in place. Here, such capping is the preferred method of remediation so as not to resuspend contaminants into the moving river. (In other conditions, a similar excavator will remove such sediment completely—hauling the polluted material up from the bottom of the river and placing it on a barge, which is tugged to a landfill or containment area designed to prevent the contaminants in the material from spreading to the surrounding environment.) Excruciatingly slow and repetitive, the rusty dinosaur, with its clamshell-bucket head filled with steel teeth, takes large bites of sand from the barge and swings to the side, dribbling material from its jaws before dunking its head into the water to release the mouthful. We watch for some time as the machine lines this once mighty river of paper with sand.

MANAGED MUD

This experience along the Fox River provides a glimpse into the highly managed, yet mostly invisible, world of sediment management in and around Great Lakes ports. The process of *adding* sediments to the riverbed to cap contaminants is analogous to a more natural process of erosion and deposition whereby eroded sediments make their way downhill with the help of moving water and eventually settle when the water velocity slows enough to allow it. In many cases this settling happens in a larger river or the lake itself, in a process of continuous shallowing. Quite often, especially within industrialized rivers, this shallowing is inconvenient, as these rivers serve as navigational routes for shipping vessels. To maintain a safe depth for passage, these routes must be continually dredged, and the material transported elsewhere. In parts of the Great Lakes—in Lake Erie, for example—some ports are so clogged with sediment that dredging operations continue almost year-round. Great Lake sediment can be characterized as anything from a toxic waste product to a valuable resource, depending on the context. In fact, many ecological systems along the nearshore require sediment for nourishment. Some areas along the shores of Lake Michigan and Lake Ontario are considered "sediment starved," as the historical erosion and longshore drift of material have been disrupted by infrastructural elements such as docks, jetties, and shoreline armor. Human actions profoundly affect the processes of erosion and require the development of management protocols. The term "sediment management" is understood to be a set of human-conceived processes necessary to generate desirable outcomes such as navigable waterways and stable shorelines.

In Green Bay, the Fox River and its shipping waterway require the annual removal, or dredging, of about 180,000 cubic yards of material—a relatively typical volume for a port of its type in the Great Lakes. This "maintenance" dredging will continue until gravity stops pulling soil downhill or until there is no need for deep shipping channels, which is to say indefinitely. The neverending cycle of dredging has stimulated myriad responses (some might call them solutions) to the big question of what to do with all that material. Decades ago, dredged sediments from shipping channels were simply cast back out into the open water and forgotten, but much of that material was toxic and negatively affected water quality and ecological health. The practice was all but abandoned in the 1960s and replaced by the containment of material within coastal structures known as confined disposal facilities, or CDFs.[2] These were at first very simple islands or peninsulas, consisting of an exterior dike wall that could be filled with pumped or placed sediments.

In Green Bay, the Renard Island CDF is an iconic example of one of these older structures. As is often the case, no one really planned for its afterlife, and once the island reached capacity it was left alone and began to support a range of colonizing plants that provide valuable habitat. To be more specific, actual plans were made, and they are continuing to be made. However, the complex administrative challenges facing an island filled with dredged sediment, in a city with little development pressure, makes any movement toward those plans very difficult. Many of the Great Lakes CDFs likewise sit quietly along the shore, too complicated to genuinely address, hosting adventitious species of all sorts, along with the occasional curious trespasser. The lima-bean-shaped Renard Island, sitting along the shore of Green Bay is no exception.

On a tour several years ago, Renard Island was an incredible rolling mass of stinging nettle, dotted with poplars and willows along

97

the rubble breakwater. It was a wholly inhospitable place, yet there was something sublime about this mound of sediment, capped with prickly nettle blowing in the wind. From this secluded place, the only sign of the city of Green Bay was an occasional scream from the Zippin Pippin roller coaster at the Bay Beach Amusement Park across the water on the mainland.

The Great Lakes CDFs were designed for a short life (that is, for a small capacity), on the assumption that material dredged from the channels would become cleaner with time and would not need to be contained. That assumption was half right; the pollution is not as bad as it once was. But planners did not anticipate that the definition of "clean" would become more restrictive over time. Environmental baselines, like the shores themselves, are continually shifting. Now the early CDFs are full, but the construction of new ones has been deemed financially infeasible at most ports. In response, Green Bay has been instrumental in demonstrating alternate strategies for dealing with these dredged sediments.

One such strategy is the processing and reuse of material at the Bayport facility, west of downtown. Bayport was the first official confined placement location in the Green Bay region and one of the first in the entire Great Lakes system. Dredged sediments were placed here beginning in 1966, and later renovations have allowed the site to continue to process material. Its capacity has been increased by a series of dewatering cells that allow water to seep out of the placed sediment and trickle back into the bay, permitting the material to consolidate and thus exposing more room for additional sediment. There are no official tours (suffice it to say that operators get few requests to visit a sediment-processing facility), but Brown County was willing to provide access when we asked. Unlike the capped and closed Renard Island, Bayport remains active through a reconfiguration toward sediment processing and reuse, allowing it to exist as a kind of operational landscape that fits in well next to the city's composting and recycling facilities. This sediment-processing model provided at Bayport has been applied elsewhere in the basin, most notably in Duluth and Cleveland, where sites have been designed to continually process dredged sediments and find alternative uses for them, including as construction material or manufactured soil.

This innovation, however, feels small compared to the work recently undertaken at Cat Island. Cat Island is the largest of a chain of historic islands that stretched across the southern portion of Green Bay, providing incredibly rich habitat as well as wave attenuation that protected urban residents and the wetlands of the Duck Creek marsh beyond.[3] These valuable islands were largely lost during a period of storms and ice movement in the 1970s. More recently, however, federal, state, and local governments have come together in a novel collaboration to address interrelated issues in this location. By 2012 they gained enough funding to begin the restoration of Cat Island, a project that was meant to restore the island's ecological functioning but also to provide a place to store dredged material. Given the complexity of this mission—one that mixes very strict habitat management with the pumping and placement of huge amounts of sediment—casual visitation is not permitted, and the site can only be toured with a guide at certain times of year. While this is an understandable policy with respect to safety, it seems a missed opportunity to connect people with their local sediments and the coastal habitats they support.

Nevertheless, adventurous visitors can walk along the road on top of the breakwater that extends from the western shore of the bay out toward the island. When the road was constructed several years ago, dump truck after dump truck unloaded giant limestone rocks, yard by yard, into the bay. All the beeping from reversing trucks and the thunder of stones rolling into the water made it hard to imagine this place as a re-created habitat. Back then it was just a stone road to nowhere. But today this walk ends at a large fence that slides down into the water on either side, prohibiting further access by the potential bird-watchers and fishing folks that might enjoy it. On either side of the breakwater road, plants have begun to organize themselves in relation to the limestone rocks and the protected environment they produce, with large stands of cattails and small poplar trees taking root in what appears to be a soilless substrate.

The initial placement of sandy material within the protected cells of the Cat Island facility created ideal conditions for the rare and loved piping plover (*Charadrius melodus*), and since then care for this bird and its habitat has guided the environmental management of the facility and preoccupied most visitors. But that agenda sometimes conflicts

99

with the site's role in sediment management. Without sediment there would be no habitat, but the sediment keeps coming and at times necessitates the disturbance of habitat, sometimes with less desirable, less sandy material. This dance, which has been going on for years, seems likely to continue as long as both agendas have a voice. And while often contentious, this co-created future, which considers economic interests and habitat creation at the same time, provides a glimpse toward a concept of adaptive negotiation that others could emulate, creating a landscape of true complexity and richness.

THE UNOFFICIAL TREE OF GREEN BAY

Our tour group for the Cat Island project includes communications folks from various state agencies. We are driven out to the site on the stone breakwater road, which is slightly submerged in some places and clogged with vegetation. The evening prior, a seiche event caused by strong winds from the north, elevated the bay's water by two feet, reaching the second-highest level ever recorded.[4] Seiche events produce some of the most dramatic water-level changes in the basin. In parts of Lake Erie, where the shallow lake runs east to west, parallel to the predominant winds, storms can pile up ten feet of water on the eastern side of the lake in Buffalo, New York, resulting in a similar drawdown of water on the western side of the lake in Toledo, Ohio. The waters from last night's seiche have receded, but the bumpy drive out on the overwashed road is unnerving, despite our tour leader's assurances that the breakwater is structurally sound. We are here to better understand the sediment and the plants that have been established at the facility, but it is clear from the discussion in the car that everyone else is here to look for piping plovers.

While our companions are glued to their scopes, trying to peep at the rare, scurrying, ground-nesting birds, we take pictures of plants and sand. Out here, trees are discouraged, as they provide perches for raptors and other birds that feed on or otherwise harass the plovers. Most of the habitat management—beyond the naming, tagging, protecting, and tracking of these scampering birds—is focused on controlling tall vegetation, and specifically the only tree that seems to truly enjoy this location, the eastern cottonwood (*Populus deltoides*).

FIGURE 4.4. Aerial View of Ken Eeurs. View looking north from above the Ken Euers Nature Area toward the Cat Island restoration project. Image by the authors.

This native pioneer species, a type of poplar, sprouts indiscriminately from piles of rocks, sand, or freshly placed mud, making it difficult to control. Toward the end of the tour, we see a sediment placement area that hosts an impressive stand of nascent poplars. We hop from the van to investigate the sea of saplings. The ground is covered with so

101

many small trees that it creates a difficult-to-discern haze across the surface of the recently placed sediment—like some type of fuzzy mud. We have a strong appreciation for the cottonwood, so seeing such an expanse of it overlaid with dialogue like "we have to get rid of all of these trees!" strikes us as comical. It is not long, however, before our tourmates—having stayed in the van to look at their cameras filled with plover photos—make it clear that our explorations of rock piles and soon-to-be-sprayed trees are of little interest, and we are reined back into the car.

On the rutted drive back across the water to the south, we see a distant line of trees, also poplars, likely one of the seeding sources for the trees we had just observed on the island. This line of poplars marks the edge of another, older postindustrial landscape, the Ken Euers Nature Area. To access the 116-acre area, we must drive through industrial zones along the western shores of Green Bay, past the Bayport facility and other sites where materials are piled up for processing and recycling. We travel through thickets of *Phragmites* and down an old gravel road to a parking lot with small signs and gates. Like so many other nature areas in the Great Lakes, Ken Euers was historically part of an extensive coastal marsh system that was later used for dumping and other industrial purposes before being abandoned and allowed to "return to nature." It was known for some time as the "Military Landfill," but that name has dropped away as the place has taken on a new identity. The city acquired the land in 1976, named it a nature area, and began to manage the site for hiking and bird-watching. Birds use the remnant ponds as marsh habitat, and an impressive allée of opportunistic cottonwood trees lines the old dike wall. What was decades ago a dump site, storing waste away from civilized eyes, now provides isolation that benefits bird-watchers, fishermen, and fans of solitude. Our visits here are always tinged with a bit of uneasiness where these wild fluctuating marsh edges collect unruly plants, animals, birds, and—judging by the abundant security cameras—people. The management of Ken Euers also feels like a response to this uneasiness. Instead of visible ecological protection or restoration efforts, most noticeable are the cameras and fences and the poplar stumps along the trail, likely removed to reduce hiding spots. We take photos and videos as we walk, attempting to capture what

FIGURE 4.5. Cottonwood Time. Time-lapse image of a cottonwood canopy. The flattened petioles of the cottonwood leaf allow it to shake and wave, creating both a visual and audible exuberance that, when experienced in large numbers, can be a formidable experience. Image by the authors.

makes this place so unique. The cottonwood trees have an obvious role in this, as our long-exposure photographs document their constant waving and rustling, making what would otherwise be a silent and still landscape a bustling mess of leaves and gnarled branches.

The eastern cottonwood that we encounter so regularly along the Great Lakes is a vigorous, water-loving pioneer plant, well adapted to the fluctuating conditions of the lake edge. Its numerous seeds are released earlier in the spring compared to those of most other species. Each tree releases more than a million of the cotton-like tufts that float through the air and accumulate into drifts of springtime "snow." While some delight in the cottonwood's showy output, others find these trees to be a nuisance and regard the cottonwoods as highly successful "weed" trees, whose weak branches are notorious for falling onto homes and automobiles. These attributes though are incredibly important to the species, its relationship to rivers and lakes, and its "pioneering" abilities. Unlike species such as oaks or pine, the cottonwood's seeds are not slow to sprout and do not wait for a perfect condition such as a fire, patch of light in a forest, or the right season; rather, cottonwoods approach their seeding through sheer numbers and swiftness. As soon as those floating seeds of the cottonwood find a newly exposed watery edge or drift, they can begin to germinate within just a few hours. In places like Cat Island, fresh piles of sediment may find themselves hosting hundreds of thousands of saplings in short order. In ideal conditions there can be as many as 400,000 cottonwood seedlings per acre.[5] This abundant strategy increases the plant's resilience in these often rough and new territories that are known for abrupt shifts in water levels and growing conditions. Some specimens will be too wet or washed away while others will be too dry; but enough will survive, and once established, they can grow at a rate exceeding ten feet per year. Such growth is assisted by adaptations such as harboring the nitrogen-fixing bacteria, *Rhizobium tropici*, in their stems allowing a young tree to acquire growth-boosting nitrogen even if its roots are on depleted soil or shifting ground.[6] The tree is not only adapted for changing landscapes but also enacts landscape changes of its own. Rapid growth quickly removes and processes water from the soil and the roots fix in mud, both stabilizing the tree and helping to reinforce the shoreline. These qualities have made poplars suitable for use in groundwater remediation, biomass creation, and shoreline stabilization. Their leaves spread out, creating new shade, shifting the adjacent microclimates. Even in their death they continue to contribute to the landscape. Their soft wood gives

FIGURE 4.6. Cottonwood Allée. Composite images exploring the spatial qualities of the cottonwood allée and cottonwood stumps at Ken Euers Nature Area. Here, one can experience walking past deeply rutted bark and stepping over stumps, which are overlaid by a long linear procession of trees along the dike. Image by the authors.

way easily to insects and bird beaks and thus gets converted to various types of habitat. The trees often fall partially at the shore, at times offering new vantage points that allow animals and people alike to perch out over the water. These fallen trees likewise can alter water flows and invite accretion, assisting in the building of the shoreline over time.

RETHINKING THE FUZZY MUD

In the field of landscape architecture, the design of the tree allée is intricately tied to influencing the experience of movement through a landscape. The lines of trees create dynamic and elegant frames that guide one along paths while emphasizing the significance of arrival to one place or departure from another. It seems fitting that out along the shore of Green Bay we find ourselves traversing a wild cottonwood allée. They may not have been planted, but the guiding presence of this allée is undeniable and arguably more influential for us than any planned and constructed design. Physically they lead us along the old dike walls of Ken Euers from which we can gaze across the bay's water to the Cat Islands where the cottonwoods have seeded their next generation. Temporally, the allées are apt guides for shoreline transformation, reminding us that our destination is not a shoreline fixed in place or overly controlled, but one that celebrates the significance and potential of change. Along river edges and shorelines, the cottonwoods have long been the harbingers of flux and adaptation, thriving with the shifts of wind, water, and mud. Helping to shape and reshape new ground, they are agents of change and designers of new landscapes. For many Indigenous peoples, cottonwoods have long been recognized and revered for their roles in harboring travelers, ushering in spring, and serving as reminders of "the connection between the stars and the earth and the sky and the universe," as written by the Crow Creek Sioux poet and writer Elizabeth Cook-Lynn.[7] As a species of change, it comes as little surprise that

▶ FIGURE 4.7. Green Bay Matrix. Collection of curated images from visits to the Green Bay region. Image by the authors.

the cottonwoods across the country are often disliked. Management of shorelines for complete control has meant a loss of the bare muddy and dynamic conditions that the cottonwoods prefer and represent. Here though, under the allées at Ken Euers, the cottonwoods usher us across the piles of discarded sediment and help us celebrate the waste as a new muddy, watery edge, a dynamic shoreline made and in the making.

INTERLUDE

THE GREAT LAKES
IN GEOLOGIC TIME

Marcia Bjornerud

Marcia Bjornerud is a professor of geosciences and environmental
studies at Lawrence University. She is the author of *Reading the Rocks:
The Autobiography of the Earth* and *Timefulness: How Thinking Like a
Geologist Can Help Save the World*. She lives in Appleton, Wisconsin.

GAZING OUT ACROSS THE VAST EXPANSE OF WATER FROM A
Great Lakes shore feels like an encounter with the eternal.
The sheer volume of the lakes suggests permanence, constan-
cy; it seems inconceivable that they have not been here forever. But
the lakes' apparent timelessness is an illusion. "Our" Great Lakes are
only the most recent of many incarnations. This makes the seemingly
simple question "How old are the Great Lakes?" surprisingly difficult
to answer.

If by the Great Lakes one means the actual water in the lakes,
they are youthful, certainly by geological and, for most of the lakes,
even human standards. The "residence" or retention time of water
in Lake Superior—the average time a molecule of H_2O stays in the
lake—is about 192 years.[1] In other words, much of the water now in
the lake fell as rain long before iron ore processors dumped tons of
asbestos mineral waste into Silver Bay in the 1950s and before the
Nipigon diversion of the 1940s. Some of the water drifted down as
snow on old-growth white pine forests of northern Wisconsin before
the clear-cutting of the 1880s and 1890s, and a fraction water still in
the lake today flowed in via tributary rivers even before Great Lakes
native nations were forced to sign the 1837 treaty that displaced them
from lands they had occupied for centuries. Lake Superior has quite a

long memory, but within our lifetimes, it will gradually forget the old days when human populations around its shores were small.

According to the metric of residence time, the other lakes are younger. Lake Michigan holds water for about 99 years, Huron for 26, Ontario for 6, and Erie for barely 3. The vast differences in residence time reflect the surface areas and volumes of the lakes as well as the magnitude and nature of their inflows and outflows, with evaporative loss being particularly dominant for the smaller, shallower lakes.

But if by the Great Lakes one means large bodies of freshwater arrayed along what is now the border between the United States and Canada, then all the lakes are on the order of thousands of years old, though not exactly in their present form. By about four thousand years ago, the Great Lakes—in what is called their "Nipissing" stage—had broad outlines we would recognize, but they were not connected in the way they are today. Superior, Michigan, and Huron were brimful, at least fifteen feet higher than modern levels, and formed a conjoined super-lake that flowed toward the Atlantic through what is now the Ottawa River Valley. Meanwhile, Erie and Ontario, without inflows from the upper lakes, were at low ebb, their surfaces more than ten feet lower than present levels. Their outlet was the Saint Lawrence, the modern exit route for the entire quintet.[2]

Still older versions of the lakes, with forms engineered by advancing ice lobes and the great moraine dams they left behind, can be recognized from abandoned shorelines at various elevations, like giant bathtub rings on the landscape. Puzzlingly, some of these rings, whose ages can be determined by carbon dating, are not horizontal, but tilted and warped. How could standing bodies of water have left slanted shorelines? The answer is that the land itself has warped over the centuries as ice encroached and retreated again, and the Earth's ductile mantle, dimly perceiving events at the surface, flowed viscously under the changing load. The Pleistocene glaciers waxed and waned at least thirty times over two million years, and we can surmise that there have been at least that many iterations of the Great Lakes. But because each new ice advance largely erased the record of the previous one, only the most recent geographies can be discerned.

Yet the Great Lakes have even deeper roots. If by the lakes one means the topographic lows that could one day hold 20 percent of the planet's freshwater, then they are far older than the Ice Age. In preglacial times, the Great Lakes Basin was a continental-scale river system whose course reflected even more ancient bedrock architecture. The three inner lakes—Michigan, Huron, and Erie—are circumscribed by the Niagara Escarpment, the bedrock ledge that marks the rim of an ancient crustal depression called the Michigan Basin. For hundreds of millions of years, this basin accumulated marine sediments, now a rich archive of life in the Paleozoic seas. The rampart of the escarpment represents some of Earth's earliest coral reefs. At times of low sea level, these reefs isolated the center of the basin from the open ocean, and great salt deposits accumulated as the briny waters evaporated. In the Anthropocene, that long-buried salt is brought back to the surface from mines deep beneath Lakes Erie and Huron to keep cars from skidding off winter roads.

Lake Superior, always claiming the superlatives, can trace its origins the farthest back in time. Its basin marks the site of an ancient volcanic rift zone, a rent in the crust from which an immense volume of basaltic lavas—more than ten miles thick below the lake bed— poured forth a billion years ago. The high density of this rock caused the crust to sag into a trough that has probably held many earlier bodies of water over the geologic eons.

How old are the Great Lakes? Very old—and very young. They are both ancient and transitory, immense and evanescent. We humans would like to think that they have always been, and always will be, as we know them. Living peaceably with these good lakes requires respect for their shape-shifting habits.

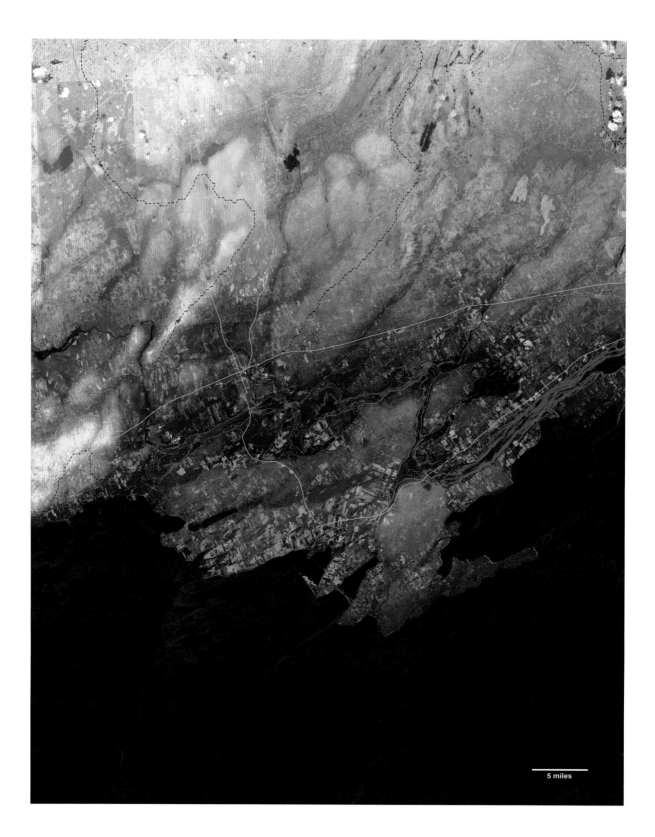

5 miles

5

BAY OF QUINTE

L EAVING A TORONTO RESTAURANT ONE EVENING, WE SPOT A
brochure advertising a quiet vacation destination two hours east
of the city. There are photos of deep-blue waters and sun-kissed
vineyards, next to boasts about the local food and crafts and the kind
of outdoor activities that appeal to weekend warriors and retirees alike.
These images are not dissimilar to other tourist-focused places in the
Great Lakes—Michigan's Traverse Bay, Ohio's Lake Erie Islands,
Wisconsin's Door County. However, neither of us has ever traveled
along the northern shore of Lake Ontario, so the brochure is our first
introduction to Prince Edward County and the Bay of Quinte. Thinking back to some of our previous experiences, we ponder: *What if it's
just fudge shops everywhere?*

As it turns out, there are more farms and cottage estates than
fudge shops. We drive the designated scenic highways, stopping to
visit small towns that proclaim to be home to the world's best this or

◄ FIGURE 5.1. Bay of Quinte. Map of the area around the Bay of Quinte, showing
general topography (contours), land use patterns, and urbanized areas (in yellow) in a
way that limits the the clear designation between land and water. The characteristic
"Z" form of the bay and the agricultural land use of Prince Edward County can be
seen here.

that. We might have preferred to hike or kayak this northern shore, but driving allows us to cover more ground while the mild weather holds. It also lets us experience the county in the way of the typical tourist, from the car window along roads that follow a heavily privatized coastline. As we drive, we scan for glimpses of water or a break in the trees that might indicate a public access point, but unfortunately we find very few. At times we park by the side of the road and sneak past mowed lawns and "no trespassing" signs to snap quick photos of the water's edge. Or, as the growing tourism economy suggests, we use our financial privilege to rent a room in a lakeside house or motel that grants us this coveted access. The water is there, but like many other highly privatized shores catering to tourism and second homes, access comes at a price.

The Bay of Quinte is a distinctive Z-shaped waterbody that separates the near island of Prince Edward County from the mainland of Ontario, Canada. Due to its peculiar shape, the bay as a whole cannot easily be comprehended at once. Whereas many of the Great Lakes bays we have explored are organized around one primary city and one main tributary, Quinte is surrounded by small towns associated with four significant tributaries that drain Ontario from the north and the west: the Trent, Moira, Salmon, and Napanee Rivers. Due to the bay's convoluted shape, at many locations along the shore land appears on all sides, making the bay seem more like a lake. And yet from other viewpoints—the Route 49 Skyway, for example—it more resembles a wide river. This visual ambiguity is appropriate; very seldom does Quinte fit the stereotype of what a bay *should* be. Watching pontoon boats and skiers skim across the water reminds us of the large reservoirs constructed by the US Army Corps of Engineers on dammed rivers in the central and western United States, touted as both flood control and recreational amenity.

LUNCHES BY THE SHORE

Near the town of Picton we rent a canoe to explore the water side of the shoreline. Paddling northeast, we hug the southern shore and note the almost cliff-like walls created by a material-handling dock on the other side of the bay. We lash a camera to the canoe in an attempt to capture the coastal edges at regular intervals as we focus on paddling. The wet and dripping oars flash into many of the photos, providing a kind of photographic metronome. At midday, tying ourselves to a long dock, we unpack our lunch and take a break. The considerable current and wind indicate that the post-lunch paddle is not going to be easy. Working in energetic bursts, we follow the shore back, documenting the many lake homes and their various docks and seawalls. At times the houses are spaced not more than ten or twenty feet apart, prompting questions about the waste and excess involved in everyone having their own private dock. At some point we are passed by a tall ship full of tourists. As the breeze propels the large ship, it also carries the sounds of their music and loud chatter. It is clear that they must have gotten a brochure very different from ours.

Recreational boaters share the bay with commercial watercraft that navigate a larger system spanning southern Ontario via the infamous Trent Severn Waterway—a 240-mile collection of 44 locks and canals that zigzag through a maze of lakes, connecting Lake Ontario to the Georgian Bay of Lake Huron. In Champlain's time, this waterway, now formalized through geoengineering, was a land-river-lake portage traveled by Indigenous peoples in canoes. That alignment seems logical when recognizing the string of lakes as the geologic intersection of Precambrian bedrock and limestone, where glacial waters carved a natural channel. It is the path of least resistance across this formidable terrain.[1] Canadian colonists imagined the route as a way to connect Lake Ontario with parts of the territory that were unexplored or sparsely populated (by Europeans), in particular the Kawartha Lakes at the upstream end of the Lake Ontario watershed.

The development of the waterway was also motivated by the only industrial function it ever really served, the production and transport of timber. Reaching deep into the Ontario forests, the canal allowed for effective timbering of large areas. It also hosted one of the early applications of the "timber slide," a Canadian invention that enabled bound rafts of squared timber to pass through rapids and waterfalls on the way to Trenton and the bay. Otherwise, the waterway was never much of an industrial success, though it has been a significant recreational amenity. Its tumultuous political history is best described in James Angus's *A Respectable Ditch*. He writes, "The discontinuous

series of events originating with the construction of a lock at Bob-caygeon . . . would comprise the longest-lasting public enterprise ever undertaken in Canada." He goes on to report that the Trent Severn Waterway, which cost $24 million when it was completed in 1920, was "used in its entirety by few except some wealthy American yachtsmen and a few adventurous Canadian canoemen."[2]

Our short walk along the Murray Canal anecdotally corroborates that account. We sit on a park bench and watch a single recreational boat drift down the enormous, quiet channel. From our seated perspective, we can see only the boat's antenna and hear the voices of those on board. This particular slice in the landscape was clearly designed for bigger boats, and this tiny vessel seems more like a mouse running down a wide hallway. The canal was built in 1889 to provide easier ship passage between the western reaches of the Bay of Quinte and Lake Ontario. This 4.5-mile-long gash through the surrounding farmland is effectively the end of the Trent Severn, now a historical landmark and tourist attraction, with boat tours, interpretative sig-nage, and other requisite markers of important yet underutilized infra-structure. But the brutally straight imposition through rolling terrain makes it impossible to deny the builders' intention to control this landscape. Despite the massive work needed to carve this razor-thin slice of water, the waterway now sits quieter than it had during its ad-venturous beginnings. On this day, we share the tightly mowed green space along the bank with a lone visitor eating lunch watching the small recreational boats slide past. The slow and tranquil experience at the canal was not an anomaly for us during our stay, but instead marked a pace of time that seemed to characterize the entire region.

SLOW GROWING

Back in the car, we move through the thick agricultural lands sur-rounding the Bay of Quinte. Field after field is crisscrossed with lines

◀ FIGURE 5.2. Oars and Shores. Composite image tracing the pace of paddling a canoe, with views of the Bay of Quinte shoreline. The monotony of rowing and the distant land are overlaid to show the temporal difference generated by scale and distance. Image by the authors.

that trace the methodical movements of tractors and tillers, harvesters and hay balers. For much of the twentieth century, Prince Edward County was an agricultural stronghold and played a major role in the early Canadian canning industry. With calcium-rich limestone soils and a temperate climate regulated by the adjacent Lake Ontario to be cooler in the summer and warmer in the winter, it was known as the "Garden County of Canada." More than seventy-five different canneries operated here between 1882 and 1996, and local peas, tomatoes, corn, pumpkin, and apples were shipped around the world.[3] Competition has since forced the canning industry into decline, but this is still one of the most hospitable agricultural regions in Canada.[4]

Over the past few decades, farmers began experimenting with a relatively new regional crop: wine grapes. While wild grapes have grown here for thousands of years, and some wine was produced in the nineteenth century, the industry did not have a notable presence until growers began to have success with the *Vitis vinifera* grape in the 1980s. The first vineyard was established in 1993, and Prince Edward County was named a Designated Viticultural Area fourteen years later. There are now well over seven hundred acres in production.[5]

In a tasting room for one of the Bay of Quinte wineries, we sip a local pinot noir as the server lines up other varietals, telling stories about the soils, the harvest, the time and process required to produce each glass. We inquire about growing methods, land management, and temperature controls. We learn that tending grapevines is different from the endeavor of dealing with more typical Great Lakes crops such as corn or soybeans. The vines require extreme care and attention, especially in a cold growing zone like Ontario, where vineyards have to be situated in specific microclimates, with gentle slopes to manage water and a north–south orientation for sun exposure.[6] Grapevines are often trained by hand, requiring the gentle fingers of a farmworker to remove new suckers at the base of the plant and curl the tendrils around the lines of a trellis. The plant and its fruit are highly sensitive to shifts in water and temperature, which influence everything from insect infestations to flavor concentrations.[7] Here in Prince Edward County, vineyard managers have the unique task of "hilling up" or burying the location on the vines where they are grafted

FIGURE 5.3. Smashed. Composite image exploring the implications and outputs of the limestone substrate of Prince Edward County. A particular soil supports vineyards, grapes, and the color of wine stains. Image by the authors.

in the winter to protect them from the cold. Growers must thus know their plants and their fields and act quickly to protect the plants from pests, drought, flooding, temperature, and other disruptions. Over the

shoulder of the person serving us, we can see what looks like a small windmill in the middle of the field, which turns out to be something like a giant fan, used to reduce frost during the growing season—taking electricity as opposed to making it.

Finding ideal microclimatic conditions for growing good grapes is challenging, and such locations are fairly limited around the bay, resulting in vineyards that are small compared to other crop-producing fields. The environmental and social benefits of small farming include less use of fertilizer and chemicals, and more support for a local culture around growing grapes and producing wine. Conveniently, those benefits increasingly tend to align with the leisure interests of people visiting from urban centers. Vineyards might be considered a "luxury" agricultural landscape, more bright and open than tightly packed rows of corn or a relentless carpet of legumes. The neatly combed parcels are often accessible to visitors and provide sweet-smelling walks and bucolic views. This is something we appreciate as we sit outside of the vineyard in colorful adirondack chairs, but then the moment is broken by a tour bus of buzzed winery tourists unloading in the parking lot behind us.

Winemakers here identify with the "slow food" and "slow tourism" movements that have spread from places like Italy and Spain to parts of the Great Lakes Basin, including Niagara in western Lake Ontario and the Finger Lakes in central New York. Following those models, the region around the Bay of Quinte is being groomed into a landscape that supports a hybrid economy of agriculture and tourism. Specialty food products, whether wine, fruit, or fish, are accompanied by experiences that commodify and enforce a "reconceptualization of time" and an emphasis on "discovery," drawing sippers, party-bus riders, and jet skiers alike.[8] These are experiences that reinforce education and engagement with the land, the seasons, and the weather, all subjects tied intrinsically to a temporal cadence quite different from what many of us are used to.

◄ FIGURE 5.4. The Dockwalker. Composite image exploring the role of docks as interfaces between land and water. In this task, all docks are the same; yet all docks are also very specific, culturally implicated, and experience-laden. Image by the authors.

Consider the moment of stepping out on a dock above the water. As you leave the stability of land, you hear the echo of your feet pounding on wood, the water lapping against that wood, and the gentle splashing of waves. On sunny days, this moment is accentuated by a shift in brightness, as the water's mirrored surface amplifies the sun's rays. The dock is a transitional infrastructure that bypasses the shallow and often "messy" area close to shore, where the water thinly covers the land, obscuring weedy plants, random organic and inorganic debris, rocky outcroppings, and muck-filled sinks. But the notion of a dock as a stable index that opposes the shifting shore is only a momentary illusion; docks themselves are also moving and messy.

To see the docks in context, perhaps it is better to be in a canoe. Paddling in and around them, their diversity material, form, and extent vary depending on era and owner. From this vantage, the stable condition of dockhood is dissolved and replaced by a ramshackle assortment of structures—decks, pontoons, piers, seawalls, and cribs—that are used to connect land and water. Some are designed with care and expertise; others appear assembled under emergency conditions with whatever materials are available. A dock does not have to be wood; any form of metal, plastic, or concrete that reaches out over the water will do. Variety is encouraged by a lack of regulations, stubborn privatization (everyone must have their *own* dock), and by the dynamic conditions generated by the coastal edge.

Much more than a house or a yard, a dock provides a very particular look into the mind and position of its creator. No matter where we travel in the Great Lakes Basin, these shoreline decisions display a wide range of attitudes toward the fluctuations of landscape and how residents respond to change. Individual docks showcase different stories, while collections of docks weave a larger local narrative about place. Docks must performatively juggle a series of demands to retain their identity. They must support human weight, provide some type of water access, and be able to accommodate variation in water level. A quick survey of a shoreline communicates that there is no universal agreement about the best way to meet those criteria. Questions such as whether a dock should float or be fixed on piers, or whether it should remain in the water through the winter or be removed to reduce ice damage, are answered differently. These demands are then overlaid by aesthetic decisions about what a dock looks like in relation to the bayside property. During our canoe tour, we observe a particularly notable example of the obsessive coordination of this relationship at one property where the elaborate brickwork from the home is smeared down to the water as paving material connecting two giant piers that frame each side of a concrete dock. The neighbor right next door, with an equally ornate home, has chosen instead a simple unassuming wooden structure hidden among weedy vegetation. In yet another location, the formal definition of a "dock" is strained by what appears to be a dump-truck load of concrete blocks jutting into the water. This focus on the docks might seem a bit silly or small to some. After all, it is just a dock, and millions of them are out there; but for us, they are real physical, material reflections of the desires, values, and understandings of the land-water-human relationship. People "love" the water, particularly those who own property along it, but what that "love" entails and how far it extends is not a given, particularly in a capitalistic system where property right and ownership are the rule. Entitlement is strong in this littoral band, a notion that is clear almost every time we are afforded a view from the water, the only fully public realm.

Back in the car, driving the shoreline roads, we seek out more water access. Occasionally a boat ramp or conservation area will let visitors reach the shore—or even walk out on the water—but such places are scarce. Eventually we find one tucked between a few "keep out" signs belonging to the neighbors, and we make our way out onto a well-worn wooden dock anchored to small metal piers that look con-siderably undersized. This is confirmed by the structure's wobbling as we head out over the water. The submerged vegetation and a discarded dock segment leaning against a bright blue outhouse indicate that the water level has risen recently. Taking off our shoes and submerging our feet, we note other influences of high water. Shrubs that once stood on the shore now dot the water as small islands.

Conditions of shoreline privatization, prevalent across the entire Great Lakes Basin, are especially salient in the Bay of Quinte. Aside from some large parks in the cities of Trenton and Belleville, the bay is mostly inaccessible to the public, edged in a thin, protective, tightly manicured lip of private land. Thus, it is not surprising that the area is also notable for its proportion of second homes. Proximity to Canada's two largest cities and parts of New York State make the location ideal for vacation and retirement property. While owners tend to think of these homes as separate from the city—a break from urban life—scholars such as Nik Luka have argued that "cottage country" (as it is commonly called) is a highly integrated component of the urban system at its periurban fringe.[9] In other words, it is not separate from the city at all, and in many cases represents the incursion of the city into territories that had previously nonurban occupants.

What compels so many people to own a cottage on a lake? Luka points us to B. K. Sandwell's observation, "The plain fact is that the Canadian will not summer anywhere except beside a lake. It does not matter much how large the lake is, nor how clean, nor what sort of odors emanate from it. A lake is a lake." Sandwell goes on to say, "Merely to dwell alongside a lake is good, but it is not everything. The true ideal of summer residence is to own a lake, so that you may dwell by it and nobody else can. . . . It is not that he is unwilling to share the use of his lake, or the fish of his lake. . . . What he wants is to be able to walk all around the blessed thing and say to himself, 'This is mine. If I like I could drain it dry and nobody could stop me.'"[10]

The opportunity to own an island within a lake affords similar feelings of complete ownership and control, and it too is possible in places like the Georgian Bay, at the western extent of the Trent Severn Waterway, where glaciers carved the bedrock into "thirty thousand islands." There, access is further privileged, as many people own islands only accessible by boat or plane.

Wolfe and Luka have studied this phenomenon in the Canadian context, and they reach similarly troubling conclusions, finding second homeownership to be a means of asserting class by owning something inessential. Understood as part of the urban system, cottage country is in continual transformation. In many places, it is now more like suburban fringe development than rural retreat. Compounding the fiction of the stable-state cottage in solitude from the city is the fiction of the stable-state shoreline environment. As the many wayward and wonky docks, platforms, and seawalls reflect, variations in water levels

126

FIGURE 5.5. Georgian Bay Islands. Aerial image of the Georgian Bay's islands, many of which are privately owned and have cottages. Image by the authors.

critically influence any built structure. Not only do these fluctuations undermine building foundations, but policywise they also challenge property owners' rights of control over the land exposed during times of low water. In theory, this newly exposed land could open up the lakeshore to a larger public, but between the "keep out" signs and the often misguided moves to build closer to the water, such action is unlikely to be accepted by the current residents.

In 2012 the Ontario legislature failed to pass the Great Lakes Shoreline Right of Passage Act, which would have allowed public pedestrian access to areas between the high and low water levels.[11] Strong opposition to the bill showed the power of landowners and their desire to control access to "their" waterfront. The dynamics are slightly different in the United States, where the public trust doctrine that governs the Great Lakes is interpreted differently by each state, but the general sentiment is very much the same. Most of the shoreline is something people want to own and control as private property to the exclusion of others.[12] Within larger cities such as Milwaukee, Chicago, Cleveland, Detroit, Buffalo, and Toronto, there are many more large, publicly accessible waterfronts. In these cities, which have more funding and more people, public lands continue to grow as cities reclaim old industrial sites. But as one leaves these cities—driving north just a couple of miles from downtown Milwaukee, for example—continuous public water access quickly dwindles to an occasional park between stately homes. For many visitors, shoreline privatization is evident not just in the Bay of Quinte, but across the entire Great Lakes Basin.

In many ways, Quinte could be held up as a regional success story. It appears to have a stable and growing economy tied to a strong sense of place and local identity. Stopping for drinks at the Drake Devonshire, a posh, art-themed boutique hotel in the small town of Wellington, we admire how the compound is tucked quietly into the residential area of the town, accessible by way of a small alley. Approaching the water's edge, the hedges and fencing become extravagant, and so do the automobiles parked nearby. Fancy designer chairs are strewn out over a wonderful rock beach surrounded by rentable suites with rates exceeding $1,000 per night. Here there are no signs, but indeed literal fences preventing hotel guests from wandering onto the surrounding properties. Feeling underdressed, we sip our expensive drinks and stare out at the water. We wonder if this experience is what the "slow food" movement aspires to. If so, then it is the likely future for other prospective regions across the basin, where tourism and privatization are not yet so extreme. A 1990 US Geological Survey report identified 83 percent of the Great Lakes shoreline as private land, and the percentage is likely higher today.[13]

Thoughts of that dwindling 17 percent linger as we sit in our fancy chairs. We cannot afford more drinks, and there is now a line of people waiting to get in. Our drinks turn out to be ironically sobering as the prized lake view is overpowered by the sights and sounds of lavish dinners and clinking wine glasses.

Leaving town the next morning, we drive back through the governmentally designated and bound Mohawk community of Tyendinaga, and the agricultural poché that fills the gaps between towns and cities. We struggle to reconcile our own access and relationships to the beautiful and bucolic landscapes of the Great Lakes with the reality that all of this, whether good or bad, well intentioned or knowingly destructive, has been produced and is governed by operations of settler colonialism, environmental control, and capitalism. Now covered with cottages and hobby farms, the landscape is being colonized a second time, driven (again) by the assumption that what was here before was empty, quiet, and open for "improvement." In many ways it is easier to decry the negative impacts of large industries with smoke-spewing factories and massive concrete pads than to come to terms with the more emotional and complicated issues embedded in the new colonizing landscapes of leisure and enjoyment. While care and joy often characterize the tourism, privatization, and local heritage of these waterfronts, the sites are also entangled with their own injustice and wastefulness.

"SLOW" DOCKS AND THE 17 PERCENT

Our time at the Bay of Quinte draws attention to a realm that landscape architects like to talk about a lot: public space. As noted before, the waters of the Great Lakes are all public, submerge your feet or sit on a boat and you are free to be in this place, but if that water recedes, or you step on dry land, this designation may disappear and more likely than not you will be "trespassing." This is the frustrating nature of governance and ownership around a vast public resource like the Great Lakes. Physically and materially, the water and land of this basin are all connected and constantly influencing one another. Yet systems of governance tend to perpetuate the drawing of lines in an attempt to regulate and control these fluctuating places.

As designers, we are interested not only in the design of public land itself but also in the use of design as an advocacy tool to find, form, and distribute more public coastal land across the Great Lakes Basin. We likewise are interested in elevating investments of money, but more important, individual investments of time that foster meaningful relationships in these collective spheres. Across the basin, public shorelines lack true collective investment and long-term responsibility. Our capitalist society prioritizes the individual. Responsibility and broader systemic understanding in land management tends to be poor when people own their own land. And while there is, in theory, more potential for the making, designing, regulating, and managing of these public lands to incorporate more benefit from collective investment, we continue to see these places reflect approaches that are the cheapest and require the least amount of "work" or "care." The places where we tend to find "care" along these shorelines in a form that simultaneously recognizes larger collectives of people, tend to be those tied to tourism. In the realm of tourism, care may be monetized and can thus be valued. From our point of view, the roles of public land and tourism could be compatible if planned and designed thoughtfully and equitably. Physically, ecologically, and socially these shorelines could benefit more species and people if they were understood and respected as collective places, even if that begins with tourism.

Consider extending how the "slow food" or "slow tourism" model that values time, broader social and ecological responsibility, education, and relation might be extended to the notion of a "slow dock." These physical moments and spaces where people traverse the littoral edge could be approached, designed, and managed as moments of intense care. This might initiate a recognition that the shifting shoreline is not something to be feared and that a healthy, sustainable relationship with the water is not one that is the most "efficient" or requires the least amount of care. Rather, a "slow dock" design might reduce fear of personal loss and elevate a community

▶ FIGURE 5.6. Bay of Quinte Matrix. Collection of curated images from around the Bay of Quinte. Image by the authors.

capacity for change that supports not only greater coastal resilience, but the relational access of more people and other species. The 17 percent should be a call to arms in what has been, to this point, a silent slipping series of losses. In the fight for public land, the tools of analysis, storytelling, and inspired physical design that landscape architects bring to the table could have serious and instrumental effect.

INTERLUDE

INTERVIEW WITH KYLE POWYS WHYTE

Kyle Powys Whyte, a Potawatomi and member of the citizen
Potawatomi Nation, is a professor of environment and sustainability
and George Willis Pack Professor at the University of Michigan
School for Environment and Sustainability, serving as a faculty
member in the environmental justice specialization.

LUTSKY / BURKHOLDER (L/B)

To start things off, perhaps we simply ask you about what comes to
your mind when you think about the Great Lakes Region.

KYLE WHYTE (KW)

When I moved here about ten years ago I was definitely hit by the
emphasis on shorelines as places that had nice views and access to water. I noticed an obsession with the pristine shoreline, with its spotless
beach and tree line. As someone who works in Indigenous studies I
was struck by how little people are interested in the actual history and
hydrology of shorelines and how they took for granted their North,
South, East, West (NSEW) orientation. I remember thinking that
would be very different from how Anishinaabe people would have understood themselves where you wouldn't necessarily have that NSEW
orientation quite the same way. Instead one's orientation would be
connected to the flow of water and the idea that one would think of
one's place in relation to a shoreline in terms of the actual transportation that water provided, the patterns of fish movement, and the edible
and medicinal plants growing nearby, among other connections. Anishinaabe people understand water as a source of livelihood and have
intimate spiritual connections to watery places like shorelines.

L/B

Perhaps in support of those insights, many of the land management decisions we have seen across the basin seldom acknowledge the idea of long-term change. As landscape architecture affiliates, we are typically tapped to respond to the immediate "problems" within this changing environment. We personally are intellectually less interested in the process of problem solving and see more value in developing methods that help us understand changing landscapes in different ways. You have also written a good deal on this topic of change, but if you are thinking about specific examples within the Great Lakes that describe how the region has changed and how it is contextualized, what would they be?

KW

In a place like Michigan or other Great Lakes states and provinces, you have a huge emphasis on tourism but also a huge emphasis on industry and industrialization. I think that that's created a misconception where people think that change has meant a moving from a condition where there wasn't much happening on shorelines, then to a state where all of sudden shorelines are industrialized or deforested, and finally a shift to the present where people have begun to clean up shorelines and use them for recreational purposes. What people miss is that the first step was not the pristine shoreline absent human footprint. Anishinaabe people and other Indigenous people of the Great Lakes had their own economies and cultures operating for generations. They saw their own economic and spiritual connections to the lakes to shorelines substantially challenged (to put it mildly) by US and Canadian colonialism.

The Anishinaabe language is well known as primarily a language of verbs and actions. Even the way you label something as a color is actually a verb in the language. So it's a very fluid language which has great emphasis on the freedom of the speaker to choose how they will articulate themselves. Scholars like Margaret Noodin do a good job of conveying some of these philosophies of the language. It is a language that can tie directly to the use of water as a primary means of transportation, the physical movement of fish, and the growing of edible and medicinal plants. One of the key changes that made it harder for a lot of Anishinaabe people to have access to the shoreline as they once did, was the plugging up of waterways and shores with dams and roadways.

When we think about change, colonialism is an act of terraforming, it is an actual act of reshaping the landscape. There was an account of a county not too far from here where the person writing in the early 1800s was talking about how originally the landscape was marshland and full of game and the native people there were thriving. But there was also a celebration about how in a short time it had become cleared, drained, and dotted with farmland. It was an act of terraforming that the settlers were convinced was perfectly normal and ethical. Similarly, we might think of cottage colonialism or even colonialism through conservation, but I think for some people it's ingrained that the pristine shoreline is ideal. These people do not realize that for a number of other groups it is deeply troubling to see large homes along shorelines or other recreational infrastructure.

If you again envision your movement across that landscape as one that's facilitated by water as opposed to paved highways, it offsets the NSEW orientation and the image of the Great Lakes. A lot of the main gathering centers for Anishinaabe people were very much related to a conception of shoreline. Sault Ste. Marie, or Bawating, is known as a place of rapids and social gathering—one reason I believe being because of the multiple shorelines that come together there.

ON ADAPTATION

L/B

You have hit on some things that relate to this, but perhaps you could speak a bit more about the culture of adaptation from your point of view.

KW

What people need to understand is that a lot of Indigenous environmental activism could be understood in the technical sense as a form of adaptation. For example, the Mother Earth Water Walk, started by

137

the late Josephine Mandamin, involved Anishinaabe grandmothers making a statement by walking around the lakes in a ceremonial fashion and being very explicit about how the lakeshore and the water were spiritually valuable and were connected to gender equity. The walk honored the fact that in Anishinaabe culture there was a responsibility vested in people based on their gender, but also that the idea of gender was fluid, more fluid than what we experience traditionally here in the United States, although things may be changing for the better.

Deborah McGregor has done a lot to document Mandamin's work. Though the knowledge is ancient, the Mother Earth Water Walk was motivated by pollution issues and was a response to the changing landscape and emphasized that each body of water had its own personality. The walk was responding to the lack of access native people have to the gathering areas near to the water, and to the insults that tourism and other industries wreak on the water and its shoreline. The emphasis on spirituality is a way Indigenous people put themselves in a space and a place to change how people think about the water. Movements like the Mother Earth Water Walk are one example, but there are many others, as Indigenous people have been active and trying to be involved in the US and Canadian political and bilateral agreements around shoreline protection. People like Frank Ettawageshik are extremely important in that process in work on the political accords affecting water quality in the Great Lakes. There's been a huge movement in the Great Lakes to protect wild rice beds and to protect fishing rights associated with Lake Superior and Lake Michigan, and many people have heard of the work of tribes like White Earth and Fond du Lac on protecting wild rice. These are all forms in which native people have engaged in activism and legal advocacy by finding ways for their own political rights to serve as tools to protect shorelines and their practices on shorelines.

L/B

We are totally enamored with the idea that there is always just a working process with this; that we must work, and adapt. There is no ideal case we are going back to, or idealized finish line, but instead it looks very constant, very fluid, or at least it feels that way.

138

I have this discussion with people, especially about concepts of wilderness and public lands, where people want there to be some form of baseline ecosystem, or a time when there were no people there. I was reading some of the work of Mishuana Goeman at UCLA, who talks about the experience of urban native people during a relocation in the 1960s. They would have to inhabit these spaces that were far away from where they were born. She quotes a poet, Esther Belin, who wrote of an experience of being native in Los Angeles and mentions that even in cases where they didn't know who the Indigenous people were, they saw the mountains and assumed that these must have been sacred to somebody. There's no presumed baseline.

L/B

The idea of the ceremony and walking the line seems important. You could imagine how this diminishes the need for a map, a device which some of us in landscape architecture have become somewhat critical of, particularly when discussing water. You do not need a map because the water is constantly moving and changing and will never be exactly where you drew it anyway.

KW

That's a good point. Things like the Water Walk point out a different way of thinking about shoreline and how we experience it. For example, if you try to walk along a shoreline, even though there are strong protections, you can't just walk along the beach the whole way. You run up into restrictions and private property. People put up fences, and visitors immediately think that if they go beyond that they'll be harmed. If alternatively, you were new to an area, you would ask who was responsible for it, or you would see how someone was taking care of it, your understanding of accessibility would be changed. This would not necessarily prevent conflict, but it does mean that people are thinking about relationships as a form of stewardship.

    I remember an occasion on Beaver Island where I was walking along the lakeshore and there was somebody whose home was under construction. They were talking about how much they liked the location on the beach and also their privacy. What does that mean? People

139

are living in ways where no one can know what they're doing, and it gives you no sense of morality. They could be taking care of the land, or they could be trashing it, either way, it is up to them alone. In this scenario, stewardship and responsibility just become about working with whatever limited space you have the legal right to work on.

L/B

Many of the landscapes we have been studying are those that tend to be leftover, not cared for, and are responding in ways that were not intended. You cannot just turn it off, even if you wanted to, and that makes them very interesting places.

KW

I am not in landscape architecture, so I may be a bit crude on this, but if you look into the histories of American conservation, much of it was tied to advocacy for a certain type of landscape. I mean John Muir for example, as depicted in the work of Eric Michael Johnson, was at the forefront of the debates about whether to continue burning practices. Muir was actually against burning while there were many white people at the time that were for burning and that insisted that's why Yosemite, with its meadows and so on, looked that way. Instead of working with the landscape, Muir suggested that that landscape just needed to be curated as space. That's part of how the national parks began—with the great naturalist and outdoors person literally trying to beautify something in the most superficial way.

L/B

I guess that's one of the reasons we are doing what we do. We believe that landscape architecture can ask or do more than just establishing an ideal spatial setup. What other Indigenous skills or practices do you see that might be associated with what we think of as landscape architecture?

KW

If I was to consider what the Indigenous equivalent of landscape architecture was, you get a list of funny skills that are not traditionally associated with landscape architecture, of which burning is a good example because it is something that has wide-ranging regional impacts and it takes a lot of skill to be able to do in order to foster and maintain a particular type of landscape. There are also people who were responsible for particular areas along shorelines, so if they were a member of a certain type of clan, they were very much about taking care of the overall habitat.

5 miles

6

MAUMEE BAY

O
N A WARM DAY IN JUNE WE MAKE OUR WAY ALONG A LONG,
thin, rocky path that juts into Maumee Bay from Cullen
Park. The water is high and choppy, and a floating mat of
sticks and logs undulates with the small, algae-laden waves. Hopping
across chunks of concrete and large mud puddles mottled with bits
of trash, we pass clumps of people sitting along the shore. The trail,
often no more than ten feet wide, is situated on an old causeway that
once stretched all the way to Grassy Island, the old sediment disposal
site at the mouth of the Maumee River. The causeway was severed
from the island decades ago, to discourage traffic to the long-filled
sediment dump. Now it has been fitted instead to a small public park
and boat launch, where it hosts a thin finger of tall trees surrounded
by the water of the bay, popular among both people and birds. We stop

◀ FIGURE 6.1. Maumee Bay. Map of the greater Maumee Bay area, showing the
general topography (contours), land use patterns, and urbanized areas (in yellow)
in a way that attempts to limit the clear designation between land and water. As a
bay, it is comparatively small, but the immense scale of the contributing agricultural
watershed of the Maumee River and the shallow bathymetry of Lake Erie's Western
Basin make the bay a concentrated area in which many important processes intermix.
Image by the authors.

143

to admire a bald eagle's nest in the high boughs of a cottonwood tree. It is a welcome sight, but not all that surprising. Birdwatchers looking for iconic eagles and small, elusive warblers know that Toledo is the place to be. Eventually the path expands, terminating in the middle of the western shore of Maumee Bay, providing a nearly 360-degree view of the Maumee River mouth, replete with the long sliver of Grassy Island, and the towering smokestacks of the Bayshore power plant in the distance. We listen to red-winged blackbirds chatter, and we watch a massive ship make its way toward the port of Toledo. From the small and swift swoop of the birds, to the slow and steady pace of the ship, we are drawn into the movement of Maumee Bay.

THE SWAMP

Historically, this bay and the lands draining into it were known as the Great Black Swamp, which stretched across a considerable portion of western Ohio and Indiana. Bounded by the Maumee on the west and the Sandusky River on the east, the swamp covered nearly a million acres.[1] It was the product of repeated glacial advances and retreats during the Pleistocene, which gouged the landscape and filled it with meltwater, creating proglacial lakes whose beds developed into swampland some fourteen thousand years ago. While the extent of those ancient lakes and the current position of the rivers help identify the swamp's general location, its exact boundaries are difficult to discern.[2] This ambiguity, defined by local, unstable variations in the intensity of wetness, made the swamp especially formidable to European settlers who were motivated to strike clear lines in the soil.

After the Revolutionary War, settlers established Connecticut's Western Reserve in what is now eastern Ohio. Pushing farther west from that outpost led them into the "fearful morass" of the Great Black Swamp.[3] Beneath the black muck, a layer of rich clay limited infiltration, allowing the shallow waters of Lake Erie to spill across the land. During the War of 1812, many soldiers died here from "marsh fever" (malaria), and others decried the constant clamor of insects and waterfowl, which kept them up at night.[4] Even the completion of the Black Swamp Road in 1827 did little to improve the area's reputation. By some accounts this was the worst road on the continent, and the side ditches were not very effective at keeping travelers unstuck.[5] The historian Harlan Hatcher observes: "The sound of horses' hoofs miring into and pulling out of this muck mile after mile all day long in the first gloom was enough to drive crazy the few hardy souls who traveled through it in wet weather. Even in the middle of the century, it was so infested with mosquitoes, so toxic with fevers and ague that few ventured to travel through it or live near it."[6]

While soldiers and settlers saw the marsh as a nuisance and a "wilderness" to be tamed, it was in fact a diverse littoral landscape that provided rich habitat, managed with care by the Indigenous people who lived there.[7] Before colonial settlement, the region was inhabited by peoples who hunted and fished in the swamp. Some lived in the region for thousands of years, and others relocated there after being pushed west from their traditional homelands.[8] While accounts of Indigenous history in this region differ, the tribes accounted for include at least the Erie, Kickapoo, Seneca, Shawnese, Wyandot, and Ottawa.[9] However, the Greenville treaties of 1795, 1814, and 1818 pushed them out so completely that today there are no federally recognized tribes or tribal lands in the state of Ohio.[10]

After forcefully removing the tribes, the colonizers' initial hesitancy toward the swamp turned into an almost militant fervor to drain it, as if it were another enemy to be conquered.[11] Malaria was eliminated, along with many of the ducks and amphibians whose resonant songs gave Toledo the nickname "Frogtown." Since the arrival of European settlers, more than 90 percent of the natural wetlands have been erased, most of them ditched, drained, and turned over to industrial agriculture and manufacturing. A few plots of marsh were saved by small factions like the famous Winous Point Hunting Club, established in 1856 just east of Maumee near Sandusky Bay.[12] Boosted by businesspeople and politicians with sway in land management decisions and a personal interest in maintaining game habitat, these groups led the work of maintaining and protecting what was left of the Great Black Swamp. Today the ecological and cultural value of the marsh is better recognized, backed nationally by the strong efforts of Ducks Unlimited and US Fish and Wildlife and locally by organizations like the Black Swamp Bird Observatory. Places like Maumee Bay State Park have re-created wetlands reminiscent of the wet past, and there

are ongoing efforts to "re-marsh" the region, turning agriculture fields back into wetlands. Nevertheless, the "Great" Black Swamp is gone for good.

Yet even now, slowness is a notable characteristic of the landscape. The clay soils of the historic swamp, mixed with sand bars from earlier glacial periods, have widened the muck-filled delta where the Maumee River empties into Lake Erie. Despite the logging, ditching, and draining of this landscape, the river still flows slowly. Only now, instead of nourishing rich wetlands, it collects nitrogen and phosphorus from the agricultural fields and deposits them at the opening of Maumee Bay, along with silt and clay from the proglacial lake beds that underlie most of the region. The fine particles of these sediments hang in the hazy water for an incredibly long time. In many of our photos of the bay, the color of the water is uncomfortably lighter than the sky, thanks to the high turbidity caused by suspended particles. In water samples we took during a summer algae bloom, the particles settled so slowly that months later, there were still tiny bits of the Great Black Swamp hovering in a small jar of Maumee Bay. While a common and natural occurrence, the abundance of these sediments in the river poses significant challenges to commercial shipping at one of the most important nodes in the Great Lakes system.

THE BUSINESS OF BOATS

It is dark and cool as we climb down the steep metal staircase into the empty belly of the ship. Our voices echo between the massive walls, and we offer up a few louder yelps and whistles to try out the acoustic capacity of this big metal void. Climbing back up the stairs, past some historical tidbit welded to the wall, we follow arrows painted on the floor to the deck. Outside, it is hot, bright, and expansive between the cabins at either end of the 617-foot-long vessel. The deck stretched over the holds has a slight arc to it, presumably useful to sheet water from the surface. We are touring the *SS Col. James M. Schoonmaker*,

◄ FIGURE 6.2. Maumee Mud. Experimentation with the sediment and muddy water collected from the Maumee Bay. Here washes, drops, masks, and stains attempt to emulate the actions of the muddy Maumee. Image by the authors.

docked permanently in downtown Toledo, where it has a new identity as part of the National Museum of the Great Lakes.

The cargo ships that crossed the lakes in the early twentieth century came in various models, including this twin-cabin version that had quarters and facilities at both the bow and the stern. An audio tour paints a narrative of a lake-bound lifestyle. Huge holding areas for bulk materials are offset by a well-designed kitchen, wood-paneled sitting rooms, and private areas for guests. At the rear is the engine room, which, judging by its size and metal surroundings, must have been an unbelievably loud place while the ship was in motion. We make our way forward to the captain's quarters, joining visitors old and young who take turns at the helm, trying to imagine working on a ship of this size, while absorbing all the facts and figures presented by the audio guide. Launched in 1911, the ship moved more than twelve thousand tons of coal between Ohio and Wisconsin on its maiden voyage. From the slowly bobbing observation deck we can see north toward the Maumee Bay. The six-mile stretch of river between downtown and the lake is filled with the guts of Toledo's industrial legacy, framed by the skyline of giant white cylinders built by petroleum companies. Pipes and conveyors stretch over the roads and rail lines, connecting the river with this field of oil cans, manufacturing facilities, and material stockpiles.

Urban development in Toledo, as in most midsize Great Lakes cities, has closely tracked the fortunes of the shipping industry. Many cities struggled in the wake of deindustrialization and have had to reposition themselves within regional markets. In Toledo, the port remains central to this process of reinvestment as its urban operations extend further, through the "More Than a Port" initiative, which includes industrial, cultural, financial, and energy-focused development projects.

Now, however, the skyline is changing. A new industrial facility broke ground in 2018, on property managed by the Port of Toledo. While under construction, the cranes loomed above an alien heap of

▶ FIGURE 6.3. Toledo to the Bay. Top image: The view from on board the Schoonmaker at the National Museum of the Great Lakes. Bottom image: Aerial view of the petroleum processing infrastructure, Grassy Island, and the Maumee Bay. Images by the authors.

metal and concrete, punctuated by pipes and stacks of all shapes. The structure looks out of place and out of proportion, even amid the other industrial infrastructure. Here iron ore mined in northern Minnesota will be converted into hot briquetted iron (HBI), which will then be shipped out to other cities to be used as fuel for blast furnaces, often for the manufacturing of steel. In this way, HBI is a product used to make other products, a go-between in the manufacturing process. This makes it an ideal symbol for the industrial condition of Toledo, which has often played a similar intermediary role, as the intermodal place where rail, road, and waterways converge.

Maumee Bay sits midway along the Great Lakes shipping network that stretches 1,500 miles from Duluth, at the far western tip of Lake Superior, out the Saint Lawrence Seaway into the Atlantic Ocean. People navigated these waters three hundred years ago in 14-foot birch-bark canoes, a vessel well suited to the shallow bays of the Great Lakes. But now many of the ports accommodate 1,000-foot lake freighters, which transport 70,000 tons of bulk cargo in one load. Historically, the cargo was dominated by large amounts of very few materials, primarily iron, coal, and grain. Iron from western mines in Minnesota, Wisconsin, and Ontario moved east to steelmaking cities such as Chicago, Cleveland, and Pittsburgh. Coal mined in Ohio and Pennsylvania was pushed back west to fuel power plants and manufacturing. Meanwhile, grain from the Central Plains left ports in Lake Superior and Lake Michigan and fed virtually the entire East Coast. The construction of the Erie Canal in the 1820s meant grain could be shipped all the way to New York City by way of the Great Lakes.

That canal was an early indicator of the intensive engineering and maintenance that would be necessary to harness the water-based resources of the Great Lakes for an industrial, mechanized future.

▶ FIGURE 6.4. The Livingstone Channel. Above: Opening Day, October 19, 1912. Image: Library of Congress, Prints & Photographs Division, Detroit Publishing Company Collection. LC-DIG-det-4a16216 (digital file from original). https://lccn. loc.gov/2016806602. Below: The dewatered Livingstone Channel under construction, taken between 1905 and 1912. Image: Library of Congress, Prints & Photographs Division, Detroit Publishing Company Collection. LC-DIG-det-4a23763 (digital file from original). https://lccn.loc.gov/2016815431.

022739 STR. WILLIAM LIVINGSTONE IN LIVINGSTONE CHANNEL. OPENING DAY, OCTOBER 19, 1912.

022006 LIVINGSTONE CHANNEL FROM LOWER LEVEL.

Although the lakes appear "natural" to most people, this is a highly modified environment, in some places controlled almost entirely by human intervention. River mouths are continually dredged to maintain deep shipping channels, and water levels are influenced by dams and locks that negotiate the 600-foot elevation change between Lake Superior and the Atlantic Ocean. The US Army Corps of Engineers manages over 600 miles of dredged navigation channels and 100 miles of breakwaters and jetties within the Great Lakes system. These extensive operations have transformed what was once a collection of glacially carved dents into a highly controlled transportation network that serves as the industrial backbone of North America.

Much of this control is asserted through three lock-and-dam systems: the Soo (on the Saint Marys River between Superior and Huron), the Welland Canal (connecting Ontario and Erie at Niagara), and the Saint Lawrence Seaway (the final stretch through Quebec to the Atlantic Ocean). But the lakes are also controlled through less visible subaqueous actions, such as continuous modifications of shipping channels. In few places has this condition been more studied and debated than in the Detroit River. The Army Corps of Engineers even went so far as to build a large physical model of the river to test strategies for reducing velocity and sediment transport.[13] Such costly explorations are feasible because the Detroit River is one of the busiest shipping routes in the United States, connecting Huron to Erie through Lake Saint Clair. No matter what is moving through the lakes or where it is going, almost all traffic passes through this highly engineered bottleneck, which looks to most people like a simple river. In 1912, the completion of the Livingstone Channel within the Detroit River was considered to be among the greatest engineering feats of the time. The project required the total dewatering of portions of the river in order to blast and excavate a large channel that would accommodate increased traffic through the dangerous passage. David Bennion and Bruce Manny have produced a rich history of this project and its environmental impacts. The findings are not surprising. Generally speaking, the desire for human control runs counter to ecological health.[14] And what may appear to be a natural, healthy river is actually a designed, constructed, and maintained conduit between strategic economic points throughout the basin.

Toledo and Maumee Bay are at the geographic center of this system, south of the Detroit River outlet, in the extremely shallow western basin of Lake Erie. Here it is not uncommon to find water depths of five feet many miles from shore, as sediment from both the Detroit and Maumee Rivers slowly fills the western end of the lake. In fact, when European colonists first reached Lake Erie, there was reportedly not a single location along its shore deep enough to naturally accommodate a shipping port.[15] In Maumee Bay this condition is exacerbated by the agricultural watershed of the Maumee River, which snakes through Ohio and Indiana and pushes loads of fine-grained sediment into the bay. To maintain the twenty-seven-foot depths required by large shipping vessels, the navigation channel for the Port of Toledo stretches some twenty miles into Lake Erie. Nearly continuous dredging produces almost one million cubic yards of material annually—the largest maintenance dredging operation in the Great Lakes system by far. Almost every time we get on the water here, we meet a mechanical dredging barge parked in the shipping channel, pulling up clay and silt from a giant underwater ditch that runs through what would naturally be around five feet of water.

For decades, that dredged material has been placed back into the lake, filling the shallow bay in areas deemed less problematic. This used to be done through "sidecasting," a process in which material was pulled from the channel and placed directly adjacent to it as the dredging ship moved along. Those historic piles of sediment are underwater, but they can still be indexed by the row of fishing boats that stretches out along the channel, tracking the fish that find those small humps attractive. Placing dredged material so near to its excavation was convenient, but the sediments tended to fall back into the channel during storm events, so now most of the dredged material is placed instead in a designated "disposal area" to the west. However, regulators would like to curtail such "open water" placement in order to reduce turbidity and nutrient disruptions to the lake ecosystem. To achieve this, state officials are exploring the use of dredged sediment for onshore uses, such as construction material, wetland creation, and as a soil amendment that could be applied back to farm fields, effectively returning the eroded soil and the nutrients it contains to where they came from.

Efforts to maintain a deep-draft harbor within a shallow, sediment-rich river mouth may seem drastic or even illogical, but they have

153

endured for more than a century. The channel keeps getting deeper as ships grow bigger and industrial activity more complex. This creates an actual rut that is difficult to escape without reconsidering the entire bulk-material transport system in North America. The tremendous economic advantages of shipping certain goods by water means this system is not likely to disappear anytime soon, leaving Toledo stuck in a loop of extreme, continual sediment management.

FOR THE BIRDS

The drive out to the Magee Marsh Wildlife Area is almost comically slow. We have no choice but to poke along at fifteen miles per hour with a pack of seemingly content bird-lovers. Drivers and passengers swivel their heads, looking for some rare migratory bird species, or so we assume. When we finally arrive at the parking lot, it is clear that we are out of our element. Suffice to say that we are well under the mean age of the visitors, and we suspect that even with another decade of savings, we could not afford the elaborate telescoping camera lenses and binoculars being hauled around. Of course we know that bird-watching is a serious hobby, even a veritable lifestyle for some, but until now we have never been this close to the scene. When we overhear an innocent inquiry about a bird species met with a sharp and judgmental comment—"It's a pine warbler!"—we resolve to not ask questions and instead turn to our phones for bird identification.

The zigzag boardwalk that rambles through the marsh is busy, but nowhere near capacity, at least compared to the photos that show the Biggest Week in American Birding event that draws ten thousand birders to the area. In those photos, the boardwalk looked more like a street festival than a wildlife trail. Today it is quieter. Deep in the wetland, we pause as a photographer frames a flitting brown bird on a branch near the boardwalk. Trying to be considerate, fearful we will scare the tiny thing away, we patiently watch as the photographer aims, focuses, and then groans when the bird moves once again. This goes on for almost ten minutes until the bird flies to a shrub on the other side, and we take advantage of the intermission to slide past, eventually making our way back toward the parking lot.

154

A walk along the beach adjacent to the parking area affords views of the sheet-pile groynes that stretch out into the lake, designed to interrupt longshore sediment transport and prevent erosion. The beach itself is a complex mix of sand, sticks, bits of tumbled wood, spent shotgun casings, and mollusk shells of all sizes. The shells collect in wracks that form large linear mounds that are nibbled away by waves, creating miniature scarps at the water's edge. They crunch and grind as we walk, each step probably equivalent to hundreds of years of wave action needed to turn shells to sand. Sand as a material is a highly contextual mix of pulverized pieces of whatever is available, whether those are shells, bits of battered coral reef, or calcified leftovers of water creatures. Today, a significant proportion of the "sand" on Great Lakes beaches is composed of shells from both quagga (*Dreissena rostriformis bugensis*) and zebra (*Dreissena polymorpha*) mussels. The mussels are invasive freshwater species from Eurasia that are unable to swim but have managed to spread from waterbody to waterbody by hitching rides in ship ballast or on the unscrubbed bottoms of fishing boats. Warm, highly trafficked Maumee Bay provides favorable conditions for these mussels, which attach themselves in clumps to structures near moving water, making shipping and its infrastructure an ideal context. As water passes around them, the mussels suck in and filter out phytoplankton and small algae. With the increased competition for these important food sources, fish numbers and diversity have declined in many of the basin's lakes and rivers. While these mollusks pose a considerable threat to the ecosystem, at this very moment they are a prime actor in what makes this place a "beach."

On our way back to Toledo we stop at the Mallard Club Wildlife Area. This wetland juts out into Lake Erie and forms the eastern shore of Maumee Bay. We were here earlier today to place our wildlife cameras and have returned to pick them up. There are no signs in the gravel parking area beyond the seasonal restrictions on hunting, and it is difficult to know if the site is even publicly accessible. But after passing through a thick mass of shrubs that line the southern areas of the marsh, we pop out into an open area of dikes and wetlands, filled with waterfowl of all kinds. Our not-so-quiet approach scares up a large flock of mallard ducks, quacking as they furiously flap their wings to get airborne. We look at each other and confirm that we are terrible

bird-watchers. Canada geese honk and glide by like low-flying aircraft before splash-landing into the wetlands, egrets and swans dot the dark water, and blackbirds perch in the stands of *Phragmites* along the dikes, singing in an asynchronous racket that is hard to speak over. (Obviously, we should not be speaking at all.) We imagine the view from above: a mass of ruffled birds trying to avoid the noisy intruders. We proceed to stomp out to the Erie shoreline, where a rock-reinforced dike protects the wetlands from the powerful waves of the lake.

Looking back across the wetland, the geometry of the dikes, ditches, and pools is evident. While it is easy to lose ourselves in the thick clumps of *Phragmites*, sumac, cattails, and willows that feel like a "wild" landscape, there are just enough pumps, gates, and drain risers to remind us that we are in a controlled environment, designed and maintained to be and stay a wetland. The Mallard Club Wildlife Area was once a private hunting club that was purchased by the state of Ohio in 1974. Now the area is managed by the Ohio Division of Wildlife, whose workers we see welding repairs to a large pump. It is hard to tell whether this landscape is really for the birds or for the hunters who like to shoot them. Around the world there is a long history of hunting lands used for wildlife preservation. The landscape architect Michael Ezban has studied landscapes such as these, particularly diked marshes used as hunting lands in western Lake Erie, and he has identified additional potential benefits including civic uses, research, and the storage of dredged sediments.[16] The idea of "polyfunctional" uses points toward a range of possibilities that these seemingly simple landscapes could have as a public amenity.

From the rock dike at the lake's edge, we can see boats lined up along the shipping channel, looking to catch walleye (*Sander vitreus*) as they head upstream to spawn. It is the spring "walleye run," and we know this small collection of boats is nothing compared to what is happening upriver on the Maumee. Side Cut Metropark is arguably

◄ FIGURE 6.5. Flight Times at the Mallard Club. Burst photography captures the various movements and paces of birds (and the occasional plane) observed at the Mallard Club and other locations around the Maumee Bay. With the timing of each burst being equal, the speed and trajectory of each subject can be measured and assessed. Image by the authors.

MAUMEE BAY

the center of that annual fishing fiasco. After a short drive we arrive at Side Cut, and in the parking lot we commit to following the fishermen with their waders and nets across the park.

We wade through a small stream and across Blue Grass Island to the banks of the Maumee River. The walk across the island is incredibly pleasant, with willows and cottonwoods speckling the landscape and worn dirt paths snaking through the tall grasses. We pass families having picnics, cyclists on the trails, and a small group hanging pinecones covered with birdseed in the park's trees. A large number of downed and tumbled trees beside the path are a sign that the entire area is occasionally flooded. The giant thorns of the native honey locust trees provide a dangerous-looking edge to the otherwise friendly bike trail. After just five minutes, we emerge through the grasses to find an almost unbelievable number of people in the river. They are lined up like soldiers, spacing themselves out as if a measured distance were required, standing on the stone bar that extends out into the river. Across the channel a row of boats, also spaced with precision, attacks the channel from the other direction. Fish are being caught and reeled in continuously, but if you have ever hooked a walleye, you know it is one of the more uninspired fights one could initiate, as the fish tends to become dead weight that has to be hauled in before splashing around a bit at the surface. This makes the quiet catching of fish go almost unnoticed. More striking are the shouts needed to re-solve tangled fishing lines, an unavoidable occurrence with this many rods and reels in such a small space.

THE ART OF STANDING STILL

This sleepy, swampy corner of Ohio provides some of the most exaggerated conditions within the Great Lakes Basin, holding multiple titles as the shallowest, warmest, fishiest, most dredged,

◀ FIGURE 6.6. Walleye Tangle. Composite image exploring the experience of fishing along the banks of the Maumee River during the Walleye run. Here, fish hang from stringers behind the fishers, anchor ropes keep the boats in place, and the constant casting of fishing lines with weighted lures all intermix to create a knot of many types (people, boats, fish, string) at one location on the river. Image by the authors.

and so on. However, very few of these dynamics are experienced directly. Reflecting on the process of standing in the river as water and fish rush by, or waiting patiently for the sighting of a rare bird, helps us understand this place of fluctuation. Many of its movements can only be appreciated if you can find a way to be still for a while. Even the sediment in a water sample we took from the bay remained suspended for months before settling to the bottom of its jar. Our collective descriptions of the Maumee Bay are largely explorations of these various movements and their own scales of operation.

Meeting any landscape takes time, patience, and a recognition that there are other times and durations beyond our own. A swan bobs in the water for hours and a blackbird flits around incessantly, both marking their time in very different ways. A hunter sits behind the blind waiting for ducks to land in the marsh. This is a very still operation of observation—right up to the point when shots are fired. So, too, the fisher's hook waiting patiently to be set. In a landscape like this—giant, slow, moist—it is encouraging to know that some communities appreciate the tempered movements of the place around them, even if they are only relating to a particular band of interest. The more residents and visitors participate in these activities, the more tuned to the particulars of the landscape the larger community becomes. As this occurs, the challenge will be how to balance the importance of use and access with ecological health and diversity in a way that allows these landscapes to remain dynamic. Perhaps it feels like something to strive for, and something that design could speak to.

This is a landscape in flux, with much of that movement being desirable for the economic and ecological health of the region, and a good deal of maintenance and care is required just to hold open spaces for that movement to occur. The blasting and dredging of shipping channels to allow for an ore freighter, the conversion of a former agriculture field into a wetland for migratory birds:

160

▶ FIGURE 6.7. Maumee Bay Matrix. Collection of curated images from visits to the Maumee Bay region. Image by the authors.

these are ongoing efforts to hold space for systems to operate and self-actualize. The work of making space for processes (landscape or otherwise) is a primary act of design that can guide us toward a more detailed exploration of what we call "curious methods."

MAUMEE BAY

INTERLUDE

INTERVIEW WITH PETER ANNIN

LUTSKY / BURKHOLDER (L/B)
Might we begin with a brief introduction to your current position?

PETER ANNIN (PA)
Sure, in 2015 I moved to Northland College, a small private liberal arts college with an environmental mission in northern Wisconsin near the shore of Lake Superior. I run a research center there called the Mary Griggs Burke Center for Freshwater Innovation. The center is unique in that it has two sides, one devoted to field research, with a focus on freshwater lakes and streams, and another that examines freshwater issues from a communication and policy standpoint. We have students doing everything from sampling and analysis of lake environments, to becoming budding journalists running around interviewing the researchers. While it is an undergraduate institution, the work is quite advanced with students involved with federal grants and such, so at times it can feel more like graduate-level work.

L/B
Could you reflect a bit on how changes around the Great Lakes, or the changes of the lakes themselves affect your work.

I might begin with the good, the bad, and the ugly. The good is that we are in an era of restoration in the Great Lakes region. This began in the Bush administration, but took off during the Obama administration and continues today. I am specifically speaking about the Great Lakes Restoration Initiative [GLRI], which has invested billions of dollars in an ecosystem that has been used and abused and run hard for more than a century. Much of this funding goes toward addressing places known as Areas of Concern and Superfund sites. These are the really chronically polluted places that are being addressed so that their waters are drinkable and swimmable again. The GLRI money is not just used for polluted sites. The largest single allotment is actually for wetlands work and restoration. It's fantastic to see Congress and the nation recognize the significant need of investing in these globally renowned water bodies that hold 20 percent of all the fresh surface water on the planet and work to bring them back closer to what they were like originally. And so, that's the good.

Then there is the bad, if you will, with climate change impacting the Great Lakes ecosystem like never before. I'm not an expert but, as a journalist and researcher, I have interviewed a lot of experts. Notably, the climate change chapter in the new edition of my book, *The Great Lakes Water Wars*, required almost 90 percent new material because the climate change situation has changed so much since the book first came out in 2006. To cut to the chase on climate change, especially by way of water levels, these levels are changing more dramatically, on a faster timescale, and setting more records—both high and low—than ever before. The historical record isn't super long, only about a century, but to give an example, in 2013 we broke the all-time record low, on Lakes Michigan and Huron, then just four years later, we set an all-time record high, on Lake Ontario, in the same water system. What we are now seeing is remarkable variability on unprecedented timescales.

The droughts are longer than they've ever been. Then we whip out of the droughts faster than ever. The water levels rise and now we're in a high water period. In 2017 and 2019 people on the shore of Lake Ontario had more water than they knew what to do with. And on the other side of the basin, Lake Superior is one of the fastest warming lakes in the world. The list goes on. That said, the climate issues in the Great Lakes region arguably are nothing compared to sea-level rise, or entire communities being burned in California. So there's this increasing conversation in the Great Lakes region about climate driven migration to the watershed because the climate issues, which are definitely here, are not as bad as having a million people lose their power because utilities are afraid of wildfires, or people being afraid of being trapped in their communities and not being able to get out before the fires. On a smaller scale this migration is happening now and we are witnessing it. For example, in a small seminar class of seven people that I taught at Northland College, two participants were climate migrants; adult students who are professionals, and had moved to the area from the West because they just got tired of all the stress about water, drought, and fires.

There was also the recent study (by Jesse Keenan, PhD, from the Harvard Graduate School of Design) that designated Duluth, Minnesota, as the most climate-resilient city in the country.[1] That does not mean that climate change is not happening in Duluth, but the problems in the study were described as less severe, making the community more adaptable. I think we can extrapolate this idea to the entire Great Lakes region as being similarly resilient to climate change in comparison to other regions.

Then, of course, you have these embayments which are often where people want to live. In these embayments the water is shallower, tends to be more productive for fishing and make the lakes more accessible to human beings. And so, if there is climate migration to the Great Lakes region it is likely that people will be locating or relocating to these same areas. But again, these areas are not immune to climate change. In 2012, Duluth had a five-hundred-year flood event that turned the streets into raging rivers, and reportedly the water was high enough for zoo animals to swim over fences and escape. This flood event created a massive sediment plume out in Lake Superior, the coldest, deepest Great Lake, causing the first-reported algal bloom on that lake. Then in 2016, ninety miles west of Duluth, Ashland, Wisconsin, experienced a thousand-year flood event with the same kind of sediment plume and another algal bloom, this time near the Apostle Islands. In 2018 the area around Houghton, Michigan, was hammered by yet another thousand-year storm causing another algal bloom that required the Apostle Islands to give water-quality warnings to its visitors and was highlighted nationally in the *New York Times*. With these events, we have entered the climate-driven algal bloom era of Lake Superior, something that people could not have fathomed before in such a cold, clear lake.

So that's the bad, but this leads us to the ugly, which relates to the algal blooms in Lake Erie. Lake Erie is the shallowest, warmest, arguably the highest developed of the five North American Great Lakes, and was declared dead in the 1970s. In the 1960s and 1970s, people were turning their backs on the lake because it stunk and looked disgusting. The Cuyahoga River caught fire many times, there just happened to be an Associated Press photographer who was there to take the pictures that went on the wire and then around the world because a river burning seemed so implausible and a clear sign that something was very wrong. However, the lake's short residence period, which causes it to respond more quickly to environmental degradation but likewise helps it heal more quickly, assisted in a remarkable rebound since the 1970s after legislations and regulations led to major changes in dumping and contamination to the point that by the late 1980s early 1990s it had a world-class fishery again.

So we had this amazing Lake Erie success story of recovery, but now, more than a decade later, we have taken a step backward again with algal blooms on the lake that are visible from space. These blooms are not only taxing to the ecosystem, but in 2014, caused a half million people in Toledo Ohio to lose access to their public drinking water. Now, we have a lake where people cannot always rely on the quality of the water because of unsustainable land use practices, namely, agriculture, but also urban water-quality issues, which in combination with these massive storm events have caused the water to now look like pea soup.

So how does all of this impact my work? Well, there are a lot of scientists, advocates, and policy experts who focus on particular subregions or individual lakes in the Great Lakes watershed, but there are not many who really concentrate on the entire watershed with its five lakes, eight states, two Canadian provinces, and many tribes and First Nations. And so for those of us who are in that basin-wide niche, as opposed to those who focus on a specific lake, state, province, or nation, the challenge is how do we communicate the wide variety of issues that the lakes face across the entire watershed? The lakes are a massive, complex interrelated system and we need people to understand the entire system as much as they can. So as a journalist, author, and speaker, I confront increasing challenges to get people to see the big picture and how it relates to their own puzzle piece on the table.

L/B

How do you get people who are typically strongly tied to local places and issues to think about the entire basin?

PA

As a storyteller I think the best way to draw people to an issue is through good storytelling. The goal is to capture them emotionally and open their eyes. I just spoke to eight hundred people in Saint Paul and I started by asking everyone who had "immersed themselves" in at least one Great Lake to stand up, and just about everyone in the room stood. Then I changed the number to two Great Lakes, and scores of people sat down. Then I changed the number to three, and then four lakes, and by the time I asked how many people had been in all five Great Lakes, there were only about twelve people still standing. You can tell an audience that the watershed is vast, but through an exercise like that, you can show them how vast it is. The basin is huge, and it is loaded with so many magical places that people should know about. The more they know, the more they will appreciate the lakes as a fragile unique interrelated watershed. Hopefully they will gain appreciation for their favorite local corner of the watershed when they see how it fits into the whole.

L/B

Perhaps our last question is about issues surrounding adaptability as a response to the changing landscapes around the basin. Do you see methods that are working well in responding to the changes you see and study? Or, in your opinion, what should the region focus on as it moves forward?

Of course, I am automatically thinking climate change adaptation things. And it's hard to find really effective ones at the moment because I think we're still kind of waking up to all of this from a public policy standpoint. For example, during the historic storms that hit the south shore of Lake Superior in 2012, 2016, and 2018, bridges and culverts were blown out by the dozens. FEMA came in and helped pay for replacement culverts, but often would not allow their size to be upgraded because officials do not want the taxpayer to be ripped of. When roads are closed, there's no time to argue, so the same-sized culverts are installed and then they get blown out in the next big storm. Is this really saving the taxpayers money? It's a lot more expensive to do it on the fly than it is to do it ahead and invest dollars that would save the taxpayer money by proactively putting in bigger culverts or other appropriately scaled infrastructure. Thankfully, we are finally starting to see changes in this area.

I am not a negative guy, but right now it is difficult to find really positive examples of adaptation in the Great Lakes region. These are not small inland lakes, they are big and charismatic, and generally speaking, people build too close to them. And when their water goes up, it goes way up, and when there is bad weather the waves are really big. If you build too close, those waves will let you know. And it's not the lakes' fault. The mistake was made years ago by people who didn't understand the dynamics of the ecosystem that they moved to and they made mistakes by building too close or buying a house that was too close during low water and not realizing what it could be like during other times.

L/B

Perhaps you could speak a bit more about the situation of climate refugees. What policies or conditions are in place to address this situation, and how do you see this changing?

PA

We need some data on how many people might come and where they will live. The main anecdotal reason we hear for people not wanting to live in the area is because the weather is cold. And while it is still going to be relatively cold, it is going to be getting warmer. One of the things the region as a whole is not very good at is long-term planning like this and what it means for green spaces, public spaces, and future communities. Planning happens within the municipal footprints, but officials are not talking across those footprints as much as they could or should. I mean certainly urban planners could project how that's going to fill out and how all the infrastructure will work, but the region is changing rapidly and we could be doing more to prepare for those changes.

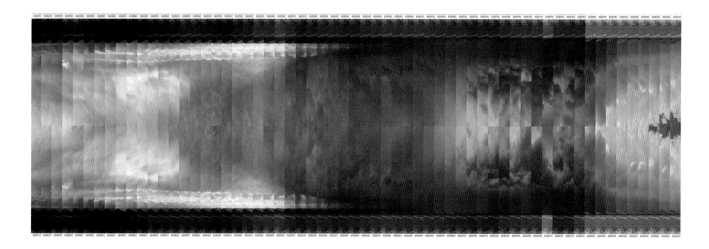

FIGURE 7.1. Curious Methods in the Gunnison Bay. Composite images tracking the movements of bodies and storms across the salt flats of the Gunnison Bay, originally published in Lutsky and Burkholder, "Curious Methods." Image by the authors.

7

CURIOUS METHODS

Knowledge is not a series of self-consistent theories that
converge toward an ideal view, it is rather an ever increasing
ocean of mutually incompatible alternatives, each single
theory, each fairy-tale, each myth is part of the collective
forcing the others into greater articulation and all of them
contributing, via this process of competition, to the development of our consciousness. Nothing is ever settled, no view
can ever be omitted from a comprehensive account."

—Paul Feyerabend, *Against Method*

MAKING SPACE FOR PLACE

Thinking about place and how we as humans come to know it can
be precarious. Places exist in the physical world, yet they are held as
constructions in the mind.[1] They are cocktails made from experience
mixed with other translated information, such as data filtered through
research or assessment protocols, or narratives generated by others.
It is helpful here to consider Derek McCormack's definition of the
"field" as "a distributed and differentiated space composed of practiced
relations between bodies, texts, technologies, and materials."[2] As the
ingredients of individual knowledge change, places are continually
formed and re-formed, often without conscious awareness. Places
are also coproduced ontologically in the physical world. What people
think of places, and how places are studied, described, and projected
upon, has tremendous bearing on what they actually are—and what
their futures may hold. There exists a loop between what is known/
thought of place and what it actually is/becomes. So to maximize the
possible futures any place may have, it should help to concurrently

maximize the ways of knowing/thinking about them. A plurality of worlds or possibilities requires a plurality of ideas and descriptions.

This book is premised on the idea that an understanding of place may be deepened by attending to how it is formed, as a thick mixture of contextual information that resists easy and objective classification. To be clear, we do not discredit all standardized methods of assessment, as they inevitably inform our ways of knowing. But it is fair to say that an overreliance on such methods, based on positivist principles of objectivity, has greatly exacerbated disconnection from place, devalued local knowledge and experience, and spread harmful notions of a human/nature divide. How designers tread in this contested landscape (intellectually and physically) is complicated by the fact that the design professions have been complicit throughout history with such views, and design practice has continued to further injustice.[3]

One way of moving forward within the practice of design, bearing in mind these concerns, involves what we have previously explored and called the "wedge."[4] As a word that operates as both a noun and a verb, the "wedge" generates an image of a physical thing in the world that performs a particular action. By "wedging" we mean an act of physical refusal against oppressive, territorializing forces. Put another way, we see our work as motivated by making space or room for other entities to self-determine—whether these are ecological systems, political activities, or social/cultural happenings. A "wedge" is designed and constructed, with due regard for function, aesthetics, and materiality (the traditional stuff of landscape practice). However, its ultimate goal is to fend off and buy time for things and systems to self-actualize, eventually making the "wedge" unnecessary. Wedging is a place-based, temporal act that ties physically constructed work to a process of becoming, obstructing swift desires for permanence that seems to underlie most constructed landscapes. It is quite hard these days to find a waterfront park in the Great Lakes Region where planned obsolescence is a central feature. More often, landscape design representations show a smattering of giant *Quercus* and *Acer* specimens, presumably emerging from nursery-picked plants supported by wire and self-watering bags, surrounded by as much lawn as possible. Everything is planned to last "forever" with minimal management beyond mowing.

The concept of wedging also extends beyond the physical landscape. As a discursive act, it can buy time for things, events, and systems. If places are both what is thought/known and what is experienced in the material world, how can space be made for other ways of thinking or knowing to self-actualize? As designers, we are responsible not only for what we make but also for what we understand and how we understand it, as these understandings inevitably inform how we work. How do operations of understanding and description create opportunity rather than finality? And beyond mere opportunity, how can understanding make room for a plurality of ideas in the attempt to provide a counterpoint to more hegemonic, reductive, and colonial ways of knowing?

A PLURALITY OF IDEAS

> Facts can be flexible friends or implacable enemies.
>
> —Kathryn Moore, *Overlooking the Visual*

Places are defined by an infinite set of narratives that coalesce around an image of the subject, and shape what is established as "true." Like any narrative construct, this truth is punched with holes, woven with anecdotes, embellished and distorted by individual and collective perceptions. Paul Feyerabend's philosophy of epistemological anarchism, which he famously described as "anything goes," suggests that we be open to all kinds of knowledge, even kinds that are counterintuitive or assembled in ways that lack empirical support. In a world without authority, how is truth established? Feyerabend argued that the acceptance of new ideas is a function of *tenacity*, or the strength of promotional activity on their behalf, and *proliferation*, or the extent of their audience.[5] It should come as no surprise that the powerful and well-funded ideas derived through rational Western science, underpinned by the "scientific method" and made rational by strings of inductive and deductive logic, exhibit both of these qualities in excess.

Feyerabend saw the growth of knowledge as a process of competitive accumulation that occurs through the simultaneous interplay of conflicting ideas. The philosopher Donna Haraway shared a similar assessment, observing that "rational knowledge is a power-sensitive conversation. Decoding and transcoding plus translation and criticism; all are necessary. Science becomes a paradigmatic model, not of closure, but of that which is contestable and contested."[6] One of the primary engines pushing this continual transformation of what we understand as true is that of experience. Naomi Oreskes, a professor of the history of science, points back nearly a century to identify the work of the philosopher William James describing how experience has a way of "boiling over" and forcing a reconsideration of previous beliefs.[7] One challenge is that the methods used to evaluate these conflicts and transformations are typically aligned with or created by Western systems of performance, precision, and predictability. In order to push back against these systems, a more equitable field upon which to discuss ideas is necessary. As designers, we may be able to create physical places that encourage such deliberation (e.g., by "wedging" them open to allow suppressed actors or assemblages to self-actualize), and this provides us a strong motivation for a particular type of practice. However, developing the field for interplay and conflict between *ideas* themselves is another task altogether.

This possible field has its roots in the concept of *plurality*. William James's series of lectures, "The Pluralistic Universe" (compiled in 1909), described pluralism as a foil to monism, which he understood as the belief that all things were connected forever. Pluralism for James constituted an acknowledgment that things were connected by degrees and in temporal configurations that were largely indeterminate. "Ever not quite has to be said of the best attempts anywhere in the universe at attaining all-inclusiveness."[8] James's conceptions of the idea of the "multiverse" and "manyness in oneness" were quite ahead of their time with respect to Western science and philosophy. More recently, support for plurality comes from social and political thinkers, such as Arturo Escobar, who are calling for a new way of "ontological design" that leverages the possibilities of social, ecological, and political autonomy and transition.[9] Escobar's work attempts to break down or call into question the binary functioning of logocentrist thought as a machine of "unfuturing" (a term drawn from Tony Fry's "defuturing"). Similar to the place/knowledge loop described earlier, Escobar illustrates a need for a relational practice of design, acknowledging that what we design in turn designs us. Put differently, there is a strong case to be made that experience matters and is foundational to knowledge, regardless of what claims to objectivity the systems of power make. Contemporary conceptions of the "pluralverse" or "a world of many worlds" lay a compelling foundation for a field of competing ideas.

As designers working with ideas of place and space, the question becomes how and what can be contributed and what additional questions may be found along the way. To this end, we will describe two different perspectives on how places could become "known"—the thick and the thin. This dualist model of coming to know and describe place has its faults. Most obviously, the model reinscribes exactly the kind of categorical thinking that we are attempting to counter. By establishing descriptions of "thick not thin" or "thin not thick" we oversimplify what might be better understood as a nonhierarchical field or gradient of possible thickness. When we use the term "thick," we are really talking about "more thick than thin," rather than a well-defined class of work. And while imperfect, these designations do provide a way to productively discuss different modalities of thinking and practice.

"Thick" and "thin" have been used recently by the landscape architect James Corner to generalize about landscape practice in the European context (where he sees a desire for thickness) and the American context (which emphasizes the thin).[10] Corner's position is a counterpoint to the landscape architect Christophe Girot's provocation that the proliferation of "thin" layered geographic information system-based analysis and photomontage have established a working method devoid of contextual specificity within American practice. In response, Corner argues, "Of course none of this means that the design methods inherent to plans, layers, photomontage and visual representation are at the root of the problem. The fact that these various techniques can be so easily misappropriated and subject to thoughtless misuse, as if by some default recipe or formula, does not render them problematic or obsolete." Corner goes on to describe several methods of working with "thin" material as a way to develop a new kind of thickness by way of "hybridization" and "cloning" as a way of justifying the kind of work Girot has called into question. If this argument leads us anywhere, it is that the attempt to categorize and generalize work as thin or thick can initiate defensive stances that attempt to wiggle from

177

those categories, but also, as we hope to show, can open up valuable avenues of discussion.

The landscape historian Thaïsa Way invokes the idea of thickness as a method for influencing the drawing of sectional illustrations as a way of "acknowledging the complex layers of history revealed in section."[11] Both Way and Corner attribute this idea of "thick description" to the anthropologist Clifford Geertz in his *Interpretation of Cultures*. Way takes Geertz's idea of "thick description" and applies it to the section, a drawing type that she feels offers particular potential in providing complex understandings of place. Geertz himself points to two disciplinary pitfalls, specific to ethnographic work, which have bearing on the understanding and description of place. The first acknowledges that the work, often described as an operation of "observation," is actually influenced and processed by the observer, and might be better defined as an "interpretation" of what was observed. So-called reality is in fact a set of explications, or even explications of explications.[12] Geertz's second pitfall describes the practice of cultural analysis, the inherent incompleteness of knowledge and the reality that more detailed information seems to lead to more incompleteness. He writes, "It is a strange science whose most telling assertions are its most tremulously based, in which to get somewhere with the matter at hand is to intensify the suspicion, both your own and that of others, that you are not quite getting it right." And while the subjects of culture and landscape here should not be carelessly conflated, if landscapes are imagined as largely cultural products, then Geertz's claim may have real implications on the practice of landscape design. There is something to be said about thickness in the idiom "the more you know, the less you know."

THIN THINKING

One approach to landscape, for which we will borrow the term "thin," involves the isolated analysis of specific landscape components or their singular relationships, often through a disciplinary framework. Instruments such as anthropological surveys or geologic samples produce highly detailed assessments along a narrow band of interest. Ask an ornithologist, a real estate developer, and a land surveyor to describe the same landscape, and you will hear three different stories, each accurate in its own way. These disciplinarily siloed stories are often motivated by the *proving* of certain facts and the disproving or ignoring of others. Things either "are" or "are not." Conditions that cannot be proven are often dismissed. In general, practitioners of thin knowledge align with Western, reductionist methods of working, supported by an institutional educational structure that prioritizes singular disciplines and expertise. With proper "tenacity" and "proliferation" these ideas can be communicated as extremely important, effectively outweighing all other perspectives. And while specific elements of a place may be deeply understood, knowledge is limited to that one dimension; hence, "thin."

Highly specialized disciplinary regimes were not a feature of the early Enlightenment, but they were its result: the product of a culture that defined progress as the positivist pursuit of total knowledge. Its revered leaders were scientists and economists. They valued causality, probability, rationality, and efficiency, and they developed a suite of quantitative tools to make the necessary measurements. Feyerabend, corresponding with his friend Imre Lakatos in 1973, lamented that science had lost its philosophical agency and had become "big business," without humanitarian concern. This "scientific" way of working was not discovered, but instead was slowly constructed and sharpened over time to become "our *creature*."[13] Escobar punctuates this thought by seeing science not only as "ineffective as an ally against authoritarianism and increasingly dependent upon market forces" but also incapable of even entering a dialogue with other forms of knowledge due to its assumed priority over them.[14] In these cases, thinness is associated with adherence to disciplinary protocols, norms, and assumptions in an attempt to demonstrate a kind of indisputable knowledge.

Encoded within these disciplinary protocols is also an agreed-upon set of values that guide the work. In one sense, the business of science has evolved along the lines of the "agrilogistic," the philosopher Timothy Morton's term for the toxic and destructive forms of land management that flourish, in spite of their flaws, because people find their logic compelling or convincing. Morton sees the agrilogistic as one of the most significant contributors to our present environmental condition. A societal majority accepts the imposition of rigid boundaries between human and nonhuman, and assumes that survival is more

179

important than quality of life.[15] For example, the many alleged benefits of modern industrial agriculture can all be reduced to one: developing ways for lots of people to live on the planet—a very pointed and *thin* objective. Within this belief system it does not matter how well people live or where, just that people survive. In this example, the values associated with the work focus entirely on quantitative success, devoid of meaning, joy, or context. Morton holds the agrilogistic responsible for patriarchy, economic inequality, and social hierarchy, as well as the negative feedback loops between human and nonhuman entities that have created an environmental crisis. The agrilogistic is also implicated in the "severing" of intellectually constructed realities from the larger set of human and nonhuman relations that make up the world.[16] We might also consider Morton's severing as a disconnection from the *places where* those relations are inscribed.

The practice of landscape architecture is not immune to such disconnection, as the possibilities that pluralistic methods might uncover are curtailed by what proliferates as a positivist agenda in landscape site assessment. Kathryn Moore describes this as a kind of "hangover" from the positivist ideas of the past and something that is endemic to our culture.[17] Disciplinary hubris has led many environmental designers to believe that they can know present conditions and predict future ones, thus making it possible to respond precisely and logically to the "problems" of any particular place. Current practice is largely devoted to the assessment and critique of landscape contexts using positivist methods shaped by a data-rich, technocratic culture.

This agenda goes back to at least the 1970s, when the landscape architect Ian McHarg and colleagues began conducting place-based assessments informed by geospatial analysis. They proposed that a site could be understood as a "layer cake" of data that would indicate feasibility for this or that use. Postmodern theories of landscape constructivism have tempered McHarg's scientific positivism, but they have not managed to shake public faith in objective site assessment, even though these methods tend to subsume different spatial and temporal realities into one space-time, and omit interactive, multiplicious, and experiential dimensions.[18] Instead, contextual analysis is still often seen as a fact-finding mission that can be marshaled to the designer's cause. The seldom-spoken but often-practiced idiom "never collect useless data" (i.e., data that could be used against you) acknowledges that site analysis is never truly objective, and it can be used to support competing or preconceived ideas. There is conversely a concern about the quantity of data that are available by way of swift present-day analytic methods. More data are not always helpful. The social and political scientist Herbert Simon once stated that "a wealth of information creates a poverty of attention, and a need to allocate that attention efficiently among the overabundance of information sources that might consume it."[19] While it can appear as a blessing, data can also drown us, with little time to properly parse it. Data collection and application must be operationalized to keep projects moving forward. But working in this way can make an attention-poor landscape analysis vulnerable to suspect claims, agendas, and worldviews, and places future possibilities at the mercy of the if–then statements of data-crunching algorithms. No information or method of processing is completely innocent, and attention to methods, findings, and responses must always be considered.

Moreover, the rise of "objective" scientific methods and research in landscape architecture has led some to imagine they can know everything about a place with little to no physical engagement. In these cases, thick information about a site is taken and flattened into lists and categories in order to tabulate relationships and perform statistical comparisons. In this process, the act of assessment actually creates and defines a place, or a version of that place. Examples of this can be seen in everything from the Sustainable Sites Initiative, which uses a point system to evaluate the performance of landscapes, to the US Army Corps *Wetland Delineation Manual*, which classifies various types of hydric landscapes as this or that kind of wetland. While these examples are well intentioned, the lists and classifications they produce describe a place in a very particular way. More than that: they *actually make the place*. Classifications and categorizations of a place strongly dictate its possible futures, and thus the futures of those human and nonhuman beings with which it is entangled. Classification becomes a clear act of Fry's "defuturing," stripping away future possibilities through acts of analysis and design.[20] In this way, the places *others make* end up *making us*. What would happen if commensurability or relatability were no longer the primary motivators of site research?

What if the interrogation itself was the point—providing an opportunity for places to push back and thicken themselves? What if *places made the lists* used to understand them?

Optimistically speaking, it seems most designers do not actually believe that place is a scientific equation to be solved.[21] Many understand that landscape problems are wicked and the truth is murky. Yet designers' methods seldom account for that murkiness, except when we are working out how to ignore it. In a statement often attributed to the philosopher of science Thomas Kuhn, "Science makes progress funeral by funeral," it is a series of mistakes, anomalies, failures, egos, and refutations, not a line of collective, well-structured discoveries.[22] If designers accept this as even somewhat true within the field of landscape, then methods are needed to locate, embrace, and protect anomalies and differences, in order to create a thicker understanding of place as *particular* not *comparable* subjects. This thick view is a way of understanding the possibilities of plurality at the landscape scale.

THE THICKENING

It is possible to envision a much *thicker*, broader, holistic way of knowing a place, attending to more of its dynamic relationships, including those that involve nonhuman entities. Such approaches are often considered an attribute of Indigenous knowledge systems, with their emphasis on active holistic relationships. The Indigenous scholar Brian Rice, a member of the Mohawk Nation, notes the need for Indigenous understandings of the environment that require active participation in a relationship with that environment, while the Oneida scholar Pam Colorado, the founder of the World Indigenous Science Network, describes Indigenous science as being like a tree with roots that "go deep into the history, body and blood of this land." Indigenous knowledge systems consistently recognize the importance of experienced knowledge, which often runs counter to the tradition of reductive Western science.[23] As the scholar Fikret Berkes states, "Indigenous knowledge pursues holism by considering a large number of variables qualitatively while Western science tends to concentrate on a small number of variables quantitatively."[24]

For centuries, Western science has attempted to dismantle the credibility of other knowledge systems. The aggressive attempts at annihilation and disruption of Indigenous lives has been and continues to be accompanied by efforts to deny sovereignty and marginalize Indigenous knowledge as mythology or folklore.[25] Without the self-proclaimed monopoly on knowledge that is Western science, there might have developed by now a more widespread, inclusive, and pluralistic way of knowing that would allow for both of these methods, and perhaps others, to coexist and supplement one another. This is precisely what the Indigenous Science Declaration for the March for Science in 2017 called for: "Let us acknowledge that there are multiple ways of knowing that play an essential role in advancing knowledge for the health of all life."[26] The botanist Robin Wall Kimmerer, an enrolled member of the Citizen Potowatomi Nation, is one of the initial signatories to the declaration, and she describes her personal journey through the Western academy in her book *Braiding Sweetgrass*. There she relays an idea from the Native scholar Greg Cajete, a Tewa of the Santa Clara Pueblo, that "we understand a thing only when we understand it with all four aspects of our being: mind, body, emotion, and spirit." In her academic training, Kimmerer writes, she was taught to recognize only "one, possibly two, of those ways of knowing: mind and body. As a young person wanting to know everything about plants, I did not question this. But it is a whole human being who finds the beautiful path." Kimmerer says that when she was finally able to "cross-pollinate" between Indigenous and Western knowledge she found a "new way of being in the world."[27]

Similarly, the geographer David Livingstone asks a series of provocative questions in his book *Putting Science in Its Place*: "To what degree was the science produced in colonies colored by the cultural policies of imperial powers?"; and "Has scientific work been used to sustain the ideology of particular groups and to promote their interests over those of others?"[28] Understood as rhetorical, Livingstone's questions point to a strategic weaponization of assumed objective knowledge for colonial and imperial ends. Livingstone tracks the development of scientific ideas as the product of particular regional contexts, arguing that "every aspect of science is open to geographic interrogation."[29] This realization of contextual contingency grinds down the cutting edge of science's agenda of pure and rational objectivity and points to a possible common ground situated around *place*.

Livingstone's examples lean heavily on what are considered Western scientific traditions, and yet even within only these examples, he finds tremendous subjectivity and regional contingency around what science is and does. If taken seriously, it necessitates a highly reflective and critical consideration of our own individual assumptions and how they shape our understanding of the world.[30]

Another pointed and critical call for "situated knowledge" was made by Donna Haraway in 1988. In her essay, Haraway outlines the paradoxical challenges of needing some form of objectivity to describe the real world while acknowledging the constructed nature of knowledge and its white masculine tendencies. Haraway proposes a form of "feminist objectivity" prioritizing partial and situated understandings that engage the negotiated and contestable discourse of science. As Haraway puts it, there is a desire to have "simultaneously an account of radical historical contingency for all knowledge claims . . . and a no-nonsense commitment to faithful accounts of a real world that can be partially shared."[31] For Haraway this partial and situated perspective is the only path to objective vision. The partial and situated nature of this perspective also makes us vulnerable and accountable, a position continually dodged by unlocatable (and thus irresponsible) knowledge claims that purport to see "everything from nowhere." Haraway alludes to some of the challenges described by Bruno Latour in his interrogation of critique, where he calls into question his role as a constructivist, engaged in the act of critical deconstruction—an act of continual subtraction. Latour confesses, "The question was never to get away from facts but closer to them, not fighting empiricism but, on the contrary, renewing empiricism."[32] Both Latour and Haraway are searching for the invaluable ground from which to lay bare the constructed nature of knowledge while possessing the empirical leverage to question something like climate change denial from a scientific and objective position.

PROBING BOTH THIS AND THAT

So, we must balance between seemingly incommensurable ideologies. How can designers respond productively to the tendency to flatten and objectify place-based understanding in a thicker, inclusive way?

A first step could be opening up to an active, messy engagement with the subject. As Haraway writes in *Staying with the Trouble*, "Alone, in our separate kinds of expertise and experience, we know both too much and too little, and so we succumb to despair or to hope and neither is a sensible attitude."[33] With respect to landscape studies, *staying with the trouble* could mean exploring the fuzzy area between ideas of places and the places themselves—very much a contested and negotiated terrain, but one that informs countless numbers of decisions by policymakers and land managers. Landscapes are ambiguous, indeterminate, dynamic, and interconnected, and we should happily and furiously explore methods of inquiry that open up those dimensions. As the philosopher Ian Hacking reminds us, "We should not expect something as motley as the growth of knowledge to be strapped to one methodology."[34]

It appears necessary to develop place-based work that synthesizes many inputs without marginalizing information collected outside an established "scientific" paradigm. Places can be *this* and *that* at the same time—they are plural assemblies that resist definition. Indeed, this condition is what makes them *places*, and not problems to be solved or facts to be proved. As Gregory Bateson observed (perhaps too hopefully), "Science Probes, it never Proves."[35] As we wrote in an earlier essay, for us, "*Probing* is a compelling term, as it implies both a curiosity and a situated context for that curiosity."[36] Unlike "analyzing," which assumes something can be completely understood, probing has both spatial and inquisitive bounds; it requires engagement, it requires experience. Yet Western scientists usually treat physical experience as a source of measurement noise and error. They develop protocols, scrub data sets, and create models to distance themselves from an embodied engagement with the world, for fear of polluting the results. This "scientific" way of working is not fundamentally wrong, as statistics and probability have brought many great advancements and understandings into being, but a more active, engaged, and inclusive process of probing could bridge a gap between ideas of place and the experienced understanding of it.

The political science philosopher William Connolly uses the term "pre-adaptation" to describe traits that are latent or suppressed within current environmental conditions, yet become evident and poignant at some future time, when they are expressed through novel interactions.[37] Connolly provides examples ranging from the evolution of the lungs in early fish into swim bladders or the use of supercomputers to exploit slow market transactions. These pre-adaptations cannot be predicted, only studied after the fact, creating an inherent unpredictability of future conditions. Places can be understood as assemblages of connected elements, including humans.[38] The pre-adaptation and unknown functions of those elements will have significant impacts on their future existence. One way to engage with and interrogate landscape would be to observe or experience how it responds to particular conditions, thus providing glimpses into its pre-adaptive characteristics. Within the landscape this can be seen in many of the preadapted species that must wait for particular conditions that may or may not ever come. The jimsonweed (*Datura stramonium*) has seeds that lay dormant under the ground for years, waiting for a shovel to turn the soil and expose them to light and air. The only way to understand how this happens is to dig a hole—you have to intervene in some way. This is not unlike the "vexing" of nature described by Francis Bacon, who proposed that the "secrets" of the natural world were more apt to reveal themselves if they were placed under the "vexations of art."[39] It is simply not good enough to find a safe place to sit back and observe phenomena; rather, it is critical to experiment and intervene. This interventionist approach demands new methods of inquiry to help see flows, connections, and interrelated agents—not individual elements *or* universal wholes.

Although we have described a process where Bacon's work could support a more engaged method of inquiry, his work also historically undergirds the experimental method that guides the most basic forms of Western science that rely on reduction. So we must search for experiential methods of inquiry and experimentation that expand opportunities, as opposed to narrowing them. Regardless of intention, all this probing, poking and vexing of landscapes still conveys a rather strong binary between subject and object, human and nature, the inquisitor and the examined. How might we as designers seek a more mutualistic understanding that underscores the interdependence or contingency between interventions and the intervened? One way forward could be inspired by Donella Meadows's provocation of *dancing*

186

with systems that was mentioned in chapter 2.[40] Instead of engaging a place or system with the desire to "discover its secrets" in the Baconian sense, what if intentions were rooted in an exchange and the additional layers of experience it brings? To extend the metaphor, imagine how the performance of different dances can teach us different things about our dancing partners—their mobility, their rhythms, their responses to our actions—and can teach us new moves in the process. Motivated by both curiosity and respect, our time together can perhaps be mutually enjoyable if we interact as equals—not with one on the examination table, subjected to inspection in the name of scientific progress or problem solving.

ACTIVE INQUIRY

Let us now return to the subject of "curious methods." Our relationships with the Great Lakes extend to our childhoods. As residents we ingested, swam, fished, and gazed upon their waters. These embodied experiences generated a relationship with these landscapes that made us feel as if we truly knew them in some form. However, now as designers, as we approach the lakes and the current critical issues surrounding them, we recognize the need to interrogate this relationship. Heeding the advice of the architecture professor Kyna Leski, we understand that "a creative process comes from displacing, disturbing, and destabilizing what you (think you) know."[41]

So, while our studies of the Great Lakes had been ongoing for years, we sought to recalibrate our methods to approaching these landscapes through a short fellowship thousands of miles away on the coastline of the Great Salt Lake. There, on the Gunnison Bay in the summer of 2016, we began our original conceptualization of what we call "curious methods."[42] During that time, we performed lighthearted experiments as a way to uncover characters within the landscape that had experiential impact on us, yet were difficult to document or understand through more standard methods of site analysis. From tracking thunderstorms to racing balloons across the salt flat, insights gathered from one experiment fed a curiosity that led to the creation of the next. We saw this work producing an alternative to what many people understand as a ubiquitous and self-similar landscape. The

187

terrain indicated on maps simply as "mud" disclosed itself to be a highly differentiated collection of interrelated landscape conditions. The landscape became much more than what the standardized systems of mapping and classification had indicated. An intuition about the landscape evolved over a period, through a process of engagement led by our experiments. Digging holes or riding bikes in circles was not the final outcome. Instead, we found a new sensibility blossoming when we were not doing the things we were "supposed" to be doing when conducting site analysis. Again, methods of inquiry are theory laden and come with their own agendas. Methods developed to find or understand one particular condition are done so at the expense of other conditions. This way of working does have value, as one might use a microscope to count troubling organisms in a drop of water or multispectral imagery to assess photosynthesis. However, this value is limited and perhaps even problematic when using the same methods to ask larger questions about the complex nature of places.

These methods arose from *a desire to develop novel understandings of pluralistic places by way of curiosity-driven question enacting.* The idea of "probing" materializes this question-enacting process in ways that can agilely adapt to the spatiotemporal evolution that characterizes many places. These methods allow us to continually modify our focus and intensity in both reactive and proactive ways.[43] Curious methods require active, physical engagement. As Michel Serres observes, "It is in the mining of coal that one learns if it is gray or black."[44] Experience becomes the driver of our expanded understanding, "boiling over" our preconceptions. Our curious methods emerge as a response to the environmental and epistemological concerns sketched above, which demand that we expand (or thicken) our understanding of place. Suppose there are other truths, other times, other histories that could unlock contextual information now suppressed or otherwise unseen. How might there develop a practice of landscape inquiry that incorporates competing theories of place? If Feyerabend is right, and knowledge is produced through a process of competitive accumulation, we need to adopt a pluralistic mode of inquiry that resists objectivity; anything else would be naive.[45]

It is possible to see the act of *dancing* with place as a form of place engagement that can help to expand the understanding of a site or landscape. Again, this activity is not motivated by *solving* or *proving*. It is an instrumental process for accumulating knowledge, and it should generate difference and dissent with the intention of thickening understanding. If consensus is ever reached—particularly in reference to what a place *is*—there is likely some agenda or actor guiding the process toward that outcome. As Feyerabend observed, "Progress has always been achieved by probing well-entrenched and well-founded forms of life with unpopular and unfounded values."[46] The "curious methods" process must thus be expansive, experimental, and creative, encompassing a tremendous range of physical, contextual engagement. All physical engagement with place (experience) generates knowledge of some kind, and those engagements can be guided or designed to contribute to the accumulation of knowledge and indicate avenues for future engagement. When dealing with a complex subject like place, revealing *truth* is not possible. Instead, questions should be used to equalize evidence and foster the tension of incommensurable knowledge systems as a way to find new insights and possibilities.[47]

The enacted question or dance is a type of experiment. As the astronomer George Darwin (a son of Charles Darwin) said, "Every once in a while, one should do a completely crazy experiment, like blowing a trumpet at tulips every morning for a month. Probably nothing will happen, but if something did happen, it would be a stupendous discovery."[48] Questions do not have to be "crazy" or even counterintuitive, but they can be. There is no reason to exclude any idea when considering something as manifold as place-based knowledge. It might be important to note that places are a specific caste of subject where question enacting can provide informative and inspirational results. Wholesale questioning of the well-established principles of gravity, or the scientifically agreed-upon existence of climate change, may not be a good use of time, but interrogating the idea and definition of "mud" in a particular context could provide tremendous insight.[49]

CONCLUSION

LOVELY DESCRIPTIONS

Poetry is the human language that can try to say what a tree or a rock or a river is, that is, to speak humanly for it, in both senses of the word "for." A poem can do so by relating the quality of an individual human relationship to a thing, a rock or river or tree, or simply by describing the thing as truthfully as possible.

Science describes accurately from outside, poetry describes accurately from inside. Science explicates, poetry implicates. Both celebrate what they describe. We need the languages of both science and poetry to save us from merely stockpiling endless "information" that fails to inform our ignorance or our irresponsibility.

—Ursula K. LeGuin, *Late in the Day*

A S LEGUIN SO ELOQUENTLY ADVOCATES AND AS WE HAVE explored throughout this book, our work of landscape tries to nestle itself as much as possible between "science" and "poetry." While we recognize the importance of experience in knowledge production, as LeGuin reminds us, our use of language and other methods of communication, whether these are drawings, photographs, or mappings, are equally critical elements in the production of our knowledge and "celebration" of landscapes and places. In addition, through this book, we are attempting to share and communicate some of this knowledge, of both place and method, with our readers. Some

◄ FIGURE C.1. Curious Methods in Action. Images of the authors exploring, experimenting, and experiencing the shorelines of the Great Lakes Region. Image by the authors.

argue that communication is the *only* stage of knowledge production, as it encodes values and participates actively in the looping process of creating a reality that in turn creates us.[1] Indeed, it should not be overlooked that the act of communication is designed. As educators we have long witnessed the potential and power of communication to create places and conjure relationships through mere projection, whether acknowledged or otherwise. A first for both of us, this book is not a passive act, but a privilege and an opportunity for us to communicate our work in a new way.

Influential to us in the examination of communication or "explanation" are the thoughts of the philosopher Peter Lipton on the process of "inference to the best explanation."[2] In this process, theories are derived through observations and the ability of those observations to explain a particular theory. But as the name of the process suggests, there is a qualitative measure to the explanation, some being better than others. Lipton advises to resist simply aligning "best" with "most likely," as is often done when selecting an explanation. Instead, Lipton proposes a layer of "loveliness" to consider the communicative power of the explanation and its persuasive possibilities. For lovely explanations to work, he says, they must not only be the most likely, but must also provide additional relevant information that enhances understanding of the subject. That said, Lipton does not call for an "anything goes" method of explanation that might support nonsensical claims. He simply draws attention to the qualitative role of explanation in support of particular ideas. Instead of just stating that this or that observation occurred, adding that it occurred in a particular place, or has a specific relationship with something else, adds to the explanatory power of the observation and the strength of the communication.

Notably, Lipton has value for us as a stepping-stone, not as a foundation, since what we are attempting is not based solely in science. However, his idea of "lovely" explanation aligns well with the previously discussed concept of "thick" descriptions of the philosopher Gilbert Ryle. For example, Ryle offers the example of a wink, a simple mechanical gesture if described through normal observation, but to understand its true meaning additional information is needed.[3] A wink requires *context*. A lovely description is one that provides richness, depth, and quality when describing places; it fills in gaps and expands possibilities instead of narrowing focus to a preferred and probable conclusion. How we communicate our observations of the landscape and experiences of place matter greatly—some are more lovely than others.

Approaches to the lovely description of place can be found across a range of disciplines, particularly in literature, design, and art. From the field of place-based writing, the book *Position Doubtful*, by the artist Kim Mahood, provides a useful model for how to communicate place in a way that enables thick and pluralistic understandings. Mahood works primarily in central Australia with Aboriginal peoples whom she befriended early in life. In the book, she shares her experiences working with these communities to map, document, and visualize their deep knowledge of the land. Notably, there is a feeling of tenuousness between Mahood and her collaborators, and between her and the place itself. "This country displaces assumptions, resists meanings," she writes. "All the ideas I've brought with me are made insubstantial by the reality of the place. The country is green and full of strange light, which makes it difficult to see."[4] Mahood's project illustrates that the many forces and feelings generated by the landscape are not easily reconciled, but it also shows that working tenaciously through the incommensurability of realities may unfold new ways of thinking and acting.

In similarly complex contexts, the landscape architects and architects Anuradha Mathur and Dilip da Cunha are known for their unique methods of engaging dynamic places. Describing their work, Mathur and da Cunha say it is "not merely critical; rather it is tentative, investigative and imaginative. We are interested in how the flux, the infinite nature of landscapes, can allow for new appropriations, new identities, and new projects, projects that work with negotiated boundaries rather than enforced limits, and that emphasize adaptation not control."[5] Their work recognizes that design propositions are inherent in the methods with which these explorations and representations are undertaken. Much of this work elegantly plays with the tensions and harmonies between forms and measurement of large-scale territories and the visceral, rhythmic, material qualities of watery edges. Their propositions are highly curated and carefully orchestrated unfoldings of conditions, both seen and unseen. Their publications and exhibitions have influenced a generation of designers (including ourselves) to recognize the importance of site-based work that empowers a more curious exploration of context and establishes it prominently within the design process. As Mathur explains, not only are the landscapes we explore negotiations, so are the methods we use to explore and interact with them.[6] In a personal conversation, she expressed some displeasure about the emphasis of so-called research in landscape practice. She instead described their way of working as more of a "digging in" to the place and project potentials, the digging leading them to future paths of study, exploration, and research—specifically grounded in processes of physical engagement with place.

Another body of work from the field of design that might resonate under the definition of lovely descriptions is that of the architect and professor, Valerio Morabito. Morabito's work weaves together a rich collection of on-site experiences, resultant memories, and possible futures into dreamlike compositions that waver between reality and fantasy—an uncanny valley of urban landscape spaces. He too has been influenced by the writing of Italo Calvino, particularly in his process that he describes as moving from "imperfection to exactitude."[7] He also considers the role of imperfection as it relates to the creation of new ideas through Darwin's theory of evolution.[8] Regardless of inspiration, Morabito's drawings offer a unique glimpse into a thinking/working process that is both curious and deeply disciplined—beginning with traces of particular places and their memories, and blossoming into sprawling speculative territories,

Such acts of engagement sometimes provide an "in" for further work. But engagement can also be the subject matter itself. The artist Andy Goldsworthy has built a career of creative interplay and physical interactions with specific environments. In the film, *Leaning into the Wind*, a long steady shot watches Goldsworthy climb horizontally through a thorny, leafless hedgerow, an onerous act tracked by slow movements, near falls, snagged clothing, and shaking branches. For a moment, backlit by a bright sky, it seems that the hedgerow has actually grown into the artist; he has become some sort of plant/person hybrid. While he is also known for physical sculptural pieces that are left to slowly degrade or emphasize climatic shifts of a place, some of the more compelling examples come from Goldsworthy more fully engaging his body in his *what-if* questions of the place. If I do this in place—do this *to* place—do this *about* place—what would happen? Might I become place? What might I learn? What might others learn? Allowing the camera to track his movement through the hedge, a rhythm of body and branch begins to develop.

CURIOUS METHODS IN ACTION

One of the more productive applications of our search for thick and lovely descriptions of landscapes and place comes by way of teaching landscape architecture. Fostering such methods of place-based understanding can have a strong impact on students, particularly in early years of landscape architecture education when students are first coming to learn about what landscape is and the role of site anaylsis in the design process. Such methods also offer a good a counterpoint to other coursework that often emphasizes more standardized methods of assessment. In this way, a good deal of our "practice" is pedagogical. Whether through design studios, seminars, or workshops, we aim to explore and illuminate different ways to learn how to learn, see how to see, and know how to know, not just for our students, but for ourselves.

Another distinction of our teaching is that it is decidedly not about problem solving, something that also motivates a good proportion of landscape architecture coursework (and professional work). This is not to say that the landscapes with which we work are not problematic, but for us the strongest potential of landscape design is its ability to critically engage and be a part of what make places special, unique, or important; and to ask open-ended questions without clear objective answers as an act of problem framing/finding or as the landscape architecture professor, Rob Holmes, calls it, "problem-setting."[9] Like Holmes, we believe there is value in teaching and practicing in ways that approach design as the proposition of *questions*, not *answers*, motivated by *places* not *problems*.

But this begs the real question, one that has lingered throughout this text and likely in the mind of the reader: What is to be done when decisions need to be made, when the "rubber hits the road"? All this expanding and pluralism sounds great up to the point when something physical in the real world needs to be designed and constructed, at

which point it appears quite unhelpful at best, and completely coun-
terproductive at worst. There is a pointed reality here that should be
addressed, as not every project is lucky enough to become a "wedge," as
described in chapter 7, although perhaps every project has the potential
to at least do a bit "wedging" if designers take it upon themselves.
This book does not seem to provide much help if you are trying to
decide between paving patterns, tree species, or fillet radius of a trendy
concrete bench. Or does it? Every decision that is made through the
process of design—whether it is the analysis of a place, the definition
of form, choice of material, or method of construction—is informed by
specific attitudes and values. This book suggests that those decisions
could open up possibilities as opposed to closing them down. They
could accept that the future will never be completely knowable, but
that uncertainty could be an opportunity. Every design is encoded
with hopes for the future; every tree specified assumes what will occur
over its lifespan. Will that future be minimized and closed down by
the decisions made, or opened and expanded to a maximum of possibilities that fight for plurality, self-actualization, change, long-term
care, and equity?

A FUTURE WITHOUT CURIOSITY

In the science-fiction short story "Twilight," written by John Campbell
in 1934, a time traveler returns from seven million years in the far
future where humans have enormous brains but are no longer able to
think creatively. Machines dedicated to survival and maintenance take
care of all needs, rendering creative thought useless. At some point
before this future, humans had created even more advanced machines
that had the capacity to think for themselves, but those machines were
turned off and eventually no one remembered how to turn them back
on. Over the course of two million years, society developed very little
and humans were disconnected from their history without the ability
to formulate questions about their place in the world. They lost all
curiosity. After discovering this omission, the time traveler locates the
"thinking" machines and sets them toward the task of creating a new
machine that will replace what was lost—a "curious" machine—before
returning to the present. This story paints a terrifying picture of a

future in which we possess tremendous quantitative knowledge yet lack the curiosity to deploy it, leading to a near-eternal life of disinterested survival. It is a curiosity-deprived future that sometimes seems a little too realistic.[10]

The current cultural focus on speed, answers, and control has marginalized curiosity and the important role of questions and uncertainty. As climate change accelerates and the world faces unprecedented population growth, there is growing fear and anxiety about what the future holds. All the systems that many were so sure they "knew," did not care about, or simply just refused to acknowledge now demand urgent attention.[11] For most of American history since colonization, changing the world and living with the landscape has meant finding new ways of controlling it. With this book though, we hope to participate in a culture that is coalescing around the idea of changing the world through asking questions of it, acknowledging uncertainty, embodying and sharing our collective knowledge, and remaining curious and humble. Seeing the landscape through the bay scale has helped us recognize the region in the local and the local in the region. It has helped us recognize contextual influences and find leverage points within environmental systems where interventions might better respect the time, material, and spirit of the human and nonhuman. We hope that this work will be helpful to others considering their own relationships to the landscapes of the Great Lakes Basin and, at the very least, that it will support the practice of staying curious and meeting landscapes without expecting answers in return.

NOTES

INTRODUCTION: GREAT LAKES PERSPECTIVES

Epigraphs: Da Cunha, *Invention of Rivers*, x. Ashworth, *Late Great Lakes*, 187.

1. Calvino, *Mr. Palomar*, 6.
2. Calvino, *Mr. Palomar*, 8.
3. Jackson, *Discovering the Vernacular Landscape*, 8.
4. Meadows, "Dancing with Systems."
5. Zumthor, *Thinking Architecture*, 65.
6. Solnit, *Field Guide.* Solnit's approach also recognizes the adaptations we have collected and acknowledges that if we want to challenge what we know we must continue to disrupt our assumptions.
7. Bennett, *Vibrant Matter*, 23–24.
8. Sundberg, "Decolonizing Posthumanist Geographies," 36. In Sundberg's piece, she notes the liberal usage of the term "we" among scholars to assume the position of the colonial authority of all. This is a critique that we have actively taken seriously throughout this text, by attempting to locate ourselves, as a pair of design thinkers, or landscape educators, or representatives of a group of actors engaged in the planning and design of coastal landscapes.
9. Tsing, *Mushroom*, 20.
10. For example, the Skywoman creation story shared by Robin Kimmerer is a prevalent Indigenous story across the Great Lakes region, which recognizes humans as part of the natural world—not as the separate entities pervasive in the Western Adam and Eve creation story.
11. Todd, "Indigenizing the Anthropocene,"
12. Donald, "On What Terms Can We Speak?" quoted in Todd, "Indigenizing the Anthropocene," 249.
13. Donald, "Forts, Curriculum and Indigenous Métissage," 6, quoted in Todd "Indigenizing the Anthropocene," 250.
14. This list was developed from the Native Lands map and is likely incomplete: accessed October 28, 2019, https://native-land.ca/

CHAPTER 1: TOWARD THE TRANSCALAR

1. Lahood, "Scale as Problem," 112.
2. Harries-Jones, *Recursive Vision*, quoted in M'Closkey and VanDerSys, *Dynamic Patterns*, 74.
3. M'Closkey and VanDerSys, *Dynamic Patterns*, 74.
4. Thün et al., *Infra Eco Logi Urbanism*, 8.

5. Latour, *Down to Earth*, 26, 40.

6. International Joint Commission, "Boundary Waters Treaty."

7. Lefebvre, *Production of Space*, 170.

8. Myers, "Ungrid-able Ecologies," 57.

9. McCormack, *Refrains for Moving Bodies*, 9.

10. Dewey, *Art as Experience,* 41.

11. Haraway, "Situated Knowledges," 590.

12. Koefoed and Simonsen, *Geographies Embodiment*, 9.

13. Latour, *Down to Earth*, 87; emphasis added.

14. Latour, *Down to Earth*, 95.

15. Haraway, *Staying with the Trouble*, 31.

16. Holling and Meffe, "Command and Control."

17. Cornell Lab of Ornithology, "Blackpoll Warbler Life History."

18. Stults et al., "Climate Change Vulnerability."

19. Holling, "Resilience and Stability," 7.

20. Holling, "Resilience and Stability," 21;emphasis added.

21. See, for example, Zolli and Healy, *Resilience*.

22. Bateson, *Mind and Nature* (1979), 9.

23. Wolff, *Delta Primer*.

24. Serres, *Natural Contract*, 30.

25. Tsing, *Mushroom*, 21.

26. Serres, *Natural Contract*, 31.

27. Bjornerud, *Timefulness*, 7.

28. Bjornerud, *Timefulness*, 8.

29. Canales, *Physicist*. This book is likely the most comprehensive account of the interactions between Einstein and Bergson.

30. Bergson, "Perception of Change." Many of Bergson's ideas on the generative power of time are expanded in clear language in this series of lectures given in Oxford.

31. Cooper, "Racial Politics of Time."

32. Rifkin, *Beyond Settler Time*.

33. Phillips, "Dismantling the Master's Clockwork Universe."

34. United Nations, "Convention on the Law of the Sea."

35. Binational, "Great Lakes Water Quality Agreement."

36. Government of Canada, "Great Lakes."

37. Milligan, "Landscape Migration."

38. Mattern, "Mapping Intelligent Agents."

39. Binational, "Great Lakes Water Quality Agreement."

40. Lutsky and Burkholder, "Curious Methods."

41. Holling, "From Complex Regions," 11, quoted in Fischer, *Climate Crisis*, 13.

CHAPTER 2: SAGINAW BAY

1. Ashworth, *Late Great Lakes*, 17.

2. Tiffin, "Collections and Researches," 61–62.

3. Michigan Department of Environmental Quality, "Salt."

4. Cohee et al., "Coal Resources," 4.

5. Fales et al., "Making the Leap," 1376.

6. Wright, "Swamp," 6.

7. Wright, "Swamp," 9.

8. Wilson, Walking Dredge, US Patent 1,289,589.

9. Michigan State University, "Geography of Michigan."

10. Freedman, "Saginaw Bay," 34.

11. Carlson Mazur, Kowalski, and Galbraith, "Assessment," 1.

12. Carlson Mazur, Kowalski, and Galbraith, "Assessment," 2.

13. Köbbing, Thevs, and Zerbe, "Utilisation of Reed," 1.

14. Moore et al., "Belowground Biomass," 612.

15. Holling and Meffe, "Command and Control."

16. Pandey and Maiti, "*Phragmites* Species," 97; and Srivastava, Kalra, and Naraian, "Environmental Perspectives."

17. Alwash, *Eden Again*, 2.

18. Köbbing, Thevs, Zerbe, "Utilisation of Reed," 1–8.

19. Hazelton et al., "*Phragmites australis* Management."

20. Hazelton et al., "*Phragmites australis* Management," 1; and Midwest Invasive Species Information Network, "Saginaw Bay Watchers."

21. Ludwig, Iannuzzi, and Esposito, "*Phragmites*," 627.

22. Reo and Ogden, "Anishnaabe Aki," 1443.

23. Reo and Ogden, "Anishnaabe Aki," 1449.

INTERLUDE: ECOLOGICAL NOVELTY AND MANAGEMENT OF THE LITTORAL ZONE

1. Boym, *Future of Nostalgia*.

2. Temple, "Nasty Necessity," 113.

CHAPTER 3: NIPIGON BAY

1. Ontario Geological Survey,"Record MD152A16NE00004," l.

2. Skrepichuk and Skrepichuk, "Vert Island Sandstone," 18.

3. Canadian Geographic, "Powered by Water."

4. Ontario Power Generation, "Northwestern Ontario Communities."

5. Waters, *Superior North Shore*, 247.

6. Scott, *Lake Nipigon*, 186.

7. Scott, *Lake Nipigon*, 194.

8. For a more detailed account of the Canadian diversions into Lake Nipigon, see Annin, *Great Lakes Water Wars*, 110–124.

9. Scott, *Lake Nipigon*, 169.

10. Findlay, "Log Torrent."

11. Kelso and Demers, *Our Living Heritage*, 93.

12. Scott, *Lake Nipigon*, 172.

13. Waters, *Superior North Shore*.

14. Waters, *Superior North Shore*.

15. Government of Canada, "Robinson Treaties."

16. Anishinabek Nation, "Robinson-Huron Treaty Rights."

17. More specifically, while many Indigenous peoples reside in these regions, very few are recognized with sovereignty over their own territories. For example, the state of Ohio does not recognize any Indigenous tribes. The last reservation in the state—the Upper Sandusky Reservation of the Wyandotte—was ceded in 1842, sending its remaining residents on their own "trail of tears" to lands in Kansas and Oklahoma. See Snook, "Wyandotte Nation."

18. McGuire, "Wiisaakodewikwe Anishinaabekwe," 217; and McGuire, "Worldviews in Transition."

19. Nelsen et al., "No Support," 3–13.

20. Nelsen et al., "Macroevolutionary Dynamics."

21. Royal Botanic Garden Edinburgh, "Lichens in the City."

22. Yoon, "Decade-Long Question."

23. Yong, "Overlooked Organisms."

24. Brandt et al., "Viability of the Lichen *Xanthoria elegans*."

25. Dybas, "Where Have All the Caribou Gone?" 862.

26. Dybas, "Where Have All the Caribou Gone?" 862.

27. Myers, "How to Grow Livable Worlds," 57–58.

28. Palmer, "Lichen Museum."

29. Gabrys, "Sensing Lichens," 352.

INTERLUDE: CULTURAL NARRATIVES OF LAKE SUPERIOR'S NORTH SHORE

The author's biography was taken in part from https://www.changinglandscapes.umn.edu/contacts.

1. Davenport and Anderson, "Getting from Sense of Place"; Henderson and Seekamp, "Battling the Tides"; Pradhananga, Davenport, and Green, "Cultural Narratives"; and Slemp et al., "Growing Too Fast."

2. Davenport, *North Shore Climate Beliefs*, 2; and Meier, Perry, and Davenport, *Perspectives on Climate*, 2.

3. Pradhananga et al., "Influence of Community Attachment," 26.

4. Tribal Adaptation Menu Team, *Dibaginjigaadeg Anishinaabe Ezhitwaad*, 54.

5. Panci et al., *Climate Change Vulnerability*, 31; and Stults et al., "Climate Change Vulnerability."

6. Fond Du Lac Band of Lake Superior Chippewa Health Impact Assessment, "Expanding the Narrative," 3.

7. Matson et al., "Transforming Research."

CHAPTER 4: GREEN BAY

1. Heesakker, "Paper Mill Industry," 82.

2. Burkholder, "Designing Dredge."

3. Port of Green Bay, "Cat Island Chain."

4. CBS Green Bay Local 5, "Flooding."

5. Stettler, *Cottonwood*, 21.

6. Stettler, *Cottonwood*, 31.

7. Lynn-Cooke, "This Is the Time."

INTERLUDE: THE GREAT LAKES IN GEOLOGIC TIME

The author's biography was found on the Princeton University Press website, https://press.princeton.edu/books/hardcover/9780691181202/timefulness.

1. United States Environmental Protection Agency, "Physical Features."

2. Lewis, Blasco, and Gareau, "Glacial Isostatic Adjustment."

CHAPTER 5: BAY OF QUINTE

1. Angus, *Respectable Ditch*, ix.

2. Angus, *Respectable Ditch*, 3.

3. Lockyer, "Uncertain Harvest."

4. Stren, "Prince Edward County," 121.

5. Holland and Smit, "Recent Climate Change," 1112.

6. Holland and Smit, "Recent Climate Change," 1112–1113.

7. Holland and Smit, "Recent Climate Change," 1112–1113.

8. Dickinson and Lumsdon, *Slow Travel*, 93 ("reconceptualization of time"); and Corvo and Matacena, "Slow Food," 98–99 ("discovery").

9. Luka, "Contested Periurban Amenity Landscapes."

10. Sandwell, "Us Amphibious Canadians."

11. Craitor, "Bill 103."

12. Norton, Meadows, and Meadows, "Drawing Lines."

13. Folger, Andreasen, and Chambers, "US Great Lakes Shoreline."

CHAPTER 6: MAUMEE BAY

1. Mitsch, "Solving Lake Erie's Harmful Algal Blooms," 406.

2. Kaatz, "Black Swamp," 2.

3. Kaatz, "Black Swamp," 14.

4. Levy, "Learning to Love the Great Black Swamp."

5. Kaatz, "Black Swamp," 12.

6. Hatcher, *Lake Erie*, 191.

7. See the Kyle Whyte interview in this volume. This is a repeated narrative across the region, as settlers assumed the land they explored was untouched wilderness as opposed to highly managed territory under the watch of other peoples.

8. Walton, "Forgotten History."

9. Library of Congress, "Indian Land Areas."

10. Snook, "Ohio's Trail of Tears." However, recent accounts of ancestors of these former Ohio tribes reveal that they are purchasing land and working to reestablish themselves in the region.

11. Egan, *Death and Life*, 215.

12. Kaufman, *Season on the Wind*, 34.

13. United States Army Corps of Engineers, *Experiments*.

14. Bennion and Manny, "Construction of Shipping Channels."

15. Hatcher, *Lake Erie*, 22.

16. Ezban, "Decoys, Dikes and Lures."

INTERLUDE: INTERVIEW WITH PETER ANNIN

1. Pierre-Louis, "Want to Escape Global Warming."

CHAPTER 7: CURIOUS METHODS

Epigraph: Feyerabend, *Against Method* (1993), 21.

1. Turnbull, "Maps, Narratives and Trails." Here Turnbull provides an overview of how spaces are constructed through experience and speculates on how to map places in adaptive ways.

2. McCormack, *Refrains for Moving Bodies*, 11.

3. The ways in which the landscape professions have been complicit in acts of direct or indirect injustice are becoming more and more evident. Whether that is something as specific as the destruction of Seneca Village, a community of freed African Americans who owned property in what was to become Central Park, or something general, such as working for a pharmaceutical company that makes billions through the opioid epidemic. There is a view of progress and growth that regularly overlooks other ethical considerations or explorations, and this problem is endemic and rather ubiquitous.

4. Burkholder and Lutsky, "Reclaiming the Littoral," 111.

5. Feyerabend, "Consolations," 211.

6. Haraway, "Situated Knowledges," 590.

7. Oreskes, *Why Trust Science?* 72.

8. James, *Pluralistic Universe*, 321.

9. Escobar, *Designs*.

10. Corner, "The Thick and the Thin."

11. Way, "Landscapes," 30.

12. Geertz, *Interpretation of Cultures*.

13. Feyerabend, "Theses on Anarchism."

14. Escobar, *Designs*, 89.

15. Morton, *Dark Ecology*, 43.

16. Morton, *Humankind*, 13.

17. Moore, *Overlooking the Visual*, 73.

18. Turnbull, "Maps, Narratives and Trails," 141.

19. Simon, "Designing Organization," 40–41.

20. Fry, *New Design Philosophy*, 11–13. For Fry the term "defuturing" has a double meaning, one is to define this act of decision making that unknowingly pushes limitations forward into our future, thus limiting what will be possible, and the other is the critical act of identifying and exposing this process of negated futures.

21. Moore, *Overlooking the Visual*, 72. Here Moore does provide the example of the Manchester Method of site analysis that attempted to do just this—develop an equation to systematize the act of site assessment.

22. Samuelson, "Reaffirming the Existence," 87.

23. Rice, "Bridging Academia," 71; and Colorado, "Bridging Native Science," 50.

24. Berkes, *Sacred Ecology*, 210. For more detail, see the Introduction to this volume, but please note that we are non-Indigenous scholars attempting to respectfully refer to knowledge systems that extend far beyond our cursory understanding.

25. Rice, "Bridging Academia," 69.

26. State University of New York, "Indigenous Science Letter."

27. Kimmerer, *Braiding Sweetgrass*, 47.

28. Livingstone, *Putting Science in Its Place*, 13.

29. Livingstone, *Putting Science in Its Place*, 14.

30. Sundberg, "Decolonizing Posthumanist Geographies." Sundberg discusses this in depth, in addition to providing a strong critique of the present posthumanist trend as a simple continuation of binary Euro-Western philosophical traditions.

31. Haraway, "Situated Knowledges," 579.

32. Latour, "Why Has Critique Run out of Steam?" 231.

33. Haraway, *Staying with the Trouble*, 4.

34. Hacking, *Representing and Intervening*, 152.

35. Bateson, *Mind and Nature*, 30.

36. Lutsky and Burkholder, "Curious Methods."

37. Connolly, *World of Becoming*, 18.

38. Bennett, *Vibrant Matter*, 23–24.

39. Bacon, *Philosophical Works*, 289; quoted in Tiles, "Experiment as Intervention," 466.

40. Meadows, *Thinking in Systems*, 165

41. Leski, *Storm of Creativity*, 13.

42. Lutsky and Burkholder, "Curious Methods."

43. Connolly, "'New Materialism.'"

44. Serres and Latour, *Conversations on Science*, 136.

45. Feyerabend, *Against Method* (2010), 14.

46. Feyerabend, "Consolations," 208.

47. Turnbull, "Maps, Narratives and Trails," 144.

48. Hacking, *Representing and Intervening*, 154. This quote is referenced by Hacking, but the original source is not provided.

49. Lutsky and Burkholder, "Curious Methods."

CONCLUSION: LOVELY DESCRIPTIONS

Epigraph: Le Guin, *Late in the Day*, foreword.

1. Two directions of note here would be first the Marshall McLuhan–inspired discussion of mapping and sensing offered by Karen M'Closkey and Keith VanDerSys in "Down to Earth." And also the general points made by Roland Barthes with respect to the role of symbology and hidden meanings within representation in *Mythologies*.

2. Lipton, "Inference."

3. Ryle, "Thinking of Thoughts."

4. Mahood, *Position Doubtful*, 36.

5. As quoted in Pevzner and Sen, "Preparing Ground."

6. Weitzman School of Design, "From the Rooftops."

7. Morabito, *City of Imagination*, 21. "Exactitude" is borrowed from Calvino, *Six Memos*, 55.

8. Morabito, *City of Imagination*, 14.

9. Holmes, "Problem with Solutions."

10. Mogen, "Re-Evaluating." Perhaps ironically, accounts of Campbell as an author and editor describe him as a crusty, science-obsessed elitist, and in many ways, lacking curiosity himself about his readership and what could constitute science fiction.

11. Bjornerud, *Timefulness*.

BIBLIOGRAPHY

Alwash, Suzanne. *Eden Again: Hope in the Marshes of Iraq.* Fullerton, CA: Tablet House, 2013.

Angus, James T. *A Respectable Ditch: A History of the Trent Severn Waterway 1833–1920.* Kingston, ON: McGill-Queens University Press, 1998.

Anishinabek Nation. "Robinson-Huron Treaty Rights 1850 and Today." Accessed November 1, 2021. http://www.anishinabek.ca/wp-content/uploads/2016/06/Robinson-Huron-Treaty-Rights.pdf.

Annin, Peter. *The Great Lakes Water Wars.* Washington, DC: Island Press, 2006.

Ashworth, William. *The Late Great Lakes: An Environmental History.* New York: Alfred A Knopf, 1986.

Bacon, Francis. *The Philosophical Works of Francis Bacon*, edited by J. M. Robertson from the edition of Ellis and Spedding. Freeport, NY: Books for Libraries Press, 1905.

Barthes, Roland. *Mythologies.* New York: Hill and Wang, 2013.

Bateson, Gregory. *Mind and Nature: A Necessary Unity.* New York: Dutton, 1979.

Bennett, Jane. *Vibrant Matter: A Political Ecology of Things.* Durham, NC: Duke University Press, 2010.

Bennion, David H. and Bruce A. Manny, "Construction of Shipping Channels in the Detroit River: History and Environmental Consequences." *U.S. Geological Survey Scientific Investigations Report* 2011–5122. Reston, VA: USGS, 2011. https://pubs.usgs.gov/sir/2011/5122/pdf/sir2011-5122.pdf.

Bergson, Henri. "The Perception of Change." In *Key Writings*, edited by Keith Pearson and John Mullarkey, 304–325. London: Bloomsbury, 2002.

Berkes, Fikret. *Sacred Ecology.* New York: Routledge, 2012.

Binational. "Great Lakes Water Quality Agreement." Annex 1 (2012). https://binational.net//wp-content/uploads/2014/05/1094_Canada-USA-GLWQA-_e.pdf.

Bjornerud, Marcia. *Timefulness: How Thinking Like a Geologist Can Help Save the World.* Princeton, NJ: Princeton University Press, 2018.

Boym Svetlana. *The Future of Nostalgia.* New York: Basic Books, 2001.

Brandt, Annette, Jean-Pierre de Vera, Silvano Onofri, and Sieglinde Ott. "Viability of the Lichen *Xanthoria elegans* and Its Symbionts after 18 Months of Space Exposure and Simulated Mars Conditions on the ISS." *International Journal of Astrobiology* 14, no. 3 (2015): 411–425. doi:10.1017/S1473550414000214.

Burkholder, Sean. "Designing Dredge: Engaging the Sediment Landscapes of the Great Lakes Basin." *Journal of Landscape Architecture* 11, no. 1 (2016): 6–17.

Burkholder, Sean, and Karen Lutsky. "Reclaiming the Littoral." In *Third Coast Atlas: Prelude to a Plan*, edited by Daniel Ibañez, Clare Lyster, Charles Waldheim, and Mason White, 106–113. New York: Actar, 2017.

Calvino, Italo. *Mr. Palomar.* San Diego: Harcourt Brace, 1985.

Calvino, Italo. *Six Memos for the Next Millennium.* Cambridge: Harvard University Press, 1988.

Canadian Geographic. "Powered by Water: From Coast to Coast." Accessed February 5, 2021. http://hydro.canadiangeographic.ca/.

Canales, Jimena. *The Physicist and the Philosopher.* Princeton, NJ: Princeton Press, 2015.

Carlson Mazur, Martha L., Kurt P. Kowalski, and David Galbraith. "Assessment of Suitable Habitat for *Phragmites australis* (Common Reed) in the Great Lakes Coastal Zone." *Aquatic Invasions* 9, no. 1 (2014): 1–19. https://doi.org/10.3391/ai.2014.9.1.01.

CBS Green Bay Local 5. "Flooding: Strong Winds, High Water and a SEICHE Create Flooding Issues." https://www.wearegreenbay.com/weather/flooding-strong-winds-high-water-and-a-seiche-create-flooding-issues/.

Cohee, George V., Ruth N. Burns, Andrew Brown, Russell A. Brant, and Dorothy Wright. "Coal Resources of Michigan." *United States Geologic Service Survey Circular* 77 (1950).

Colorado, Pam. "Bridging Native Science and Western Science." *Convergence* 21, no. 2–3 (1988): 49–68.

Connolly, William E. "The 'New Materialism' and the Fragility of Things." *Millennium* 41, no. 3 (2013): 399–412.

Connolly, William E. *A World of Becoming.* Durham, NC: Duke University Press, 2011.

Cooper, Britney. "The Racial Politics of Time." October 2016, *TEDWomen*, Video, 12:21. https://www.ted.com/talks/brittney_cooper_the_racial_politics_of_time.

Cornell Lab of Ornithology. "Blackpoll Warbler Life History." Accessed October 11, 2019. https://www.allaboutbirds.org/guide/Blackpoll_Warbler/lifehistory.

Corner, James. "The Thick and the Thin of It." In *Thinking the Contemporary Landscape*, edited by Christophe Girot and Dora Imhof, 117–135. Princeton, NJ: Princeton Architectural Press, 2017.

Corvo, Paolo, and Raffaele Matacena. "Slow Food in Slow Tourism." In *Slow Tourism, Food and Cities: Pace and the Search for the "Good Life,"* edited by Michael Clancy, 95–109. New York: Routledge, 2018.

Craitor, Kim. "Bill 103: Great Lakes Shoreline Right of Passage Act." *Legislative Assembly of Ontario*, 2012. https://www.ola.org/en/legislative-business/bills/parliament-40/session-1/bill-103.

Da Cunha, Dilip. *The Invention of Rivers: Alexander's Eye and Ganga's Descent.* Philadelphia: University of Pennsylvania Press, 2019.

Davenport, M. A. *North Shore Climate Beliefs Report.* St. Paul: Center for Changing Landscapes, University of Minnesota, 2018.

Davenport, M. A., and D. H. Anderson. "Getting from Sense of Place to Place-based Management: An Interpretive Investigation of Place Meanings and Perceptions of Landscape Change." *Society and Natural Resources* 18, no. 7 (2005): 625–641.

Dewey, John. *Art As Experience.* New York: Perigee Books, 1980.

Dickinson, Janet, and Leslie Lumsdon. *Slow Travel and Tourism.* New York: Earthscan, 2010.

Donald, Dwayne. "Forts, Curriculum and Indigenous Métissage: Imagining Decolonization of Aboriginal-Canadian Relations in Educational Contexts." *First Nations Perspectives* 2, no. 1 (2009): 1–24.

Donald, Dwayne. "On What Terms Can We Speak?" Lecture at the University of Lethbridge, 2010. www.vimeo.com/15264558.

Dybas, Cheryl Lyn. "Where Have All the Caribou Gone? Population Viability Analysis May Offer Answers." *BioScience* 62, no. 10 (October 2012): 862–866. https://doi.org/10.1525/bio.2012.62.10.4.

Egan, Dan. *The Death and Life of the Great Lakes*. New York, London: W. W. Norton, 2017.

Escobar, Arturo. *Designs for the Pluralverse*. Durham, NC: Duke University Press, 2017.

Ezban, Michael, "Decoys, Dikes and Lures: Polyfunctional Landscapes of Waterfowl Hunting." *Studies in the History of Gardens & Designed Landscapes* 33 (2013): 193–207. 10.1080/14601176.2013.820921.

Fales, Mary, Randal Dell, Matthew E. Herbert, Scott P. Sowa, Jeremiah Asher, Glenn O'Neil, Patrick J. Doran and Benjamin Wickerham. "Making the Leap from Science to Implementation: Strategic Agricultural Conservation in Michigan's Saginaw Bay Watershed." *Journal of Great Lakes Research* 42, no. 6 (2016): 1372–1385. https://doi.org/10.1016/j.jglr.2016.09.010.

Feyerabend, Paul. *Against Method*. London: Verso, 1993.

Feyerabend, Paul. *Against Method*. London: Verso, 2010.

Feyerabend, Paul. "Consolations for the Specialist." In *Criticism and the Growth of Knowledge*, edited by Imre Lakatos and Alan Musgrave, 197–230. London: Cambridge University Press, 1970.

Feyerabend, Paul. "Theses on Anarchism." In *For and Against Method*, edited by Matteo Motterlini, 113–118. Chicago: University of Chicago Press, 1999.

Findlay, D.K. "The Log Torrent." *Macleans Magazine*, September 15, 1944.

Fischer, Frank. *Climate Crisis and the Democratic Prospect: Participatory Governance in Sustainable Communities*. Oxford: Oxford University Press, 2017.

Fond Du Lac Band of Lake Superior Chippewa Health Impact Assessment. "Expanding the Narrative of Tribal Health: The Effects of Wild Rice Water Quality Rule Changes on Tribal Health." *Fond Du Lac Band of Lake Superior Chippewa Resource Management Division* (2018). http://www.fdlrez.com/rm/downloads/WQSHIA.pdf.

Folger, D. W., Christian Andreasen, and M. J. Chambers. "US Great Lakes Shoreline Mapping Plan." *National Oceanic and Atmospheric Administration* Open File Report 90–97 (1990). https://pubs.usgs.gov/of/1990/0097/report.pdf.

Freedman, Paul L. "Saginaw Bay: An Evaluation of Existing and Historical Conditions." United States Environmental Protection Agency, Report No. EPA-905/9-74-003 (1974).

Fry, Tony. *A New Design Philosophy: An Introduction to Defuturing*. Sydney: UNSW Press, 1999.

Gabrys, Jennifer. "Sensing Lichens: From Ecological Microcosms to Environmental

Subjects." *Third Text* 32, no. 2–3 (May 4, 2018): 350–367. https://doi.org/10.1080/095 28822.2018.1483884.

Geertz, Clifford. *The Interpretation of Cultures: Selected Essays.* New York: Basic Books, 1973.

Government of Canada. "Great Lakes: Areas of Concern." Accessed December 2, 2021. https://www.canada.ca/en/environment-climate-change/services/great-lakes -protection/areas-concern.html.

Government of Canada. "Robinson Treaties and Douglas Treaties (1850–1854)." Accessed March 30, 2021. https://rcaanc-cirnac.gc.ca/eng/1360945974712/15446199 09155.

Hacking, Ian. *Representing and Intervening.* Cambridge: Cambridge University Press, 1983.

Haraway, Donna. "Situated Knowledges: The Science Question in Feminism and the Privilege of Partial Perspective." *Feminist Studies* 14, no. 3 (1988): 575–599.

Haraway, Donna. *Staying with the Trouble: Making Kin in the Chthulucene.* Durham & London: Duke University Press, 2016.

Harries-Jones, Peter. *A Recursive Vision: Ecological Understanding and Gregory Bateson.* Toronto: University of Toronto Press, 1995.

Hatcher, Harlan. *Lake Erie (The American Lake Series).* New York: Bobbs Merrill, 1945.

Hazelton, Eric L. G., Thomas J. Mozdzer, David M. Burdick, Karin M. Kettenring, and Dennis F. Whigham. "*Phragmites australis* Management in the United States: 40 Years of Methods and Outcomes." *AoB PLANTS* 6 (2014): 10–13. https://doi .org/10.1093/aobpla/plu001.

Heesakker, Dorothy. "The Paper Mill Industry in the Lower Fox River Valley, Wisconsin 1872–1890." MA thesis, Loyola University, 1965.

Henderson, M., and E. Seekamp. "Battling the Tides of Climate Change: The Power of Intangible Cultural Resource Values to Bind Place Meanings in Vulnerable Historic Districts." *Heritage* 1, no. 2 (2018): 220–238.

Holland, Tara, and Barry Smit. "Recent Climate Change in the Prince Edward County Winegrowing Region, Ontario, Canada: Implications for Adaptation in a Fledgling Wine Industry." *Regional Environmental Change* 14, no. 3 (2014): 1109–1121.

Holling, C. S. "From Complex Regions to Complex Worlds." *Ecology and Society* 9, no. 1 (2004): art. 11. https://doi.org/10.5751/ES-00612-090111.

Holling, C. S. "Resilience and Stability of Ecological Systems." *Annual Review of Ecology and Systematics* 4 (1973): 1–23.

Holling, C. S., and Gary K. Meffe. "Command and Control and the Pathology of Natural Resource Management." *Conservation Biology* 10, no. 2 (April 1996): 328–337.

Holmes, Rob. "The Problem with Solutions." *Places Journal* (July 2020). https://doi.org/ 10.22269/200714.

International Joint Commission. "Boundary Waters Treaty of 1909." Accessed December 1, 2021. https://www.ijc.org/en/boundary-waters-treaty-1909.

Jackson, John Brinckerhoff. *Discovering the Vernacular Landscape.* New Haven, CT: Yale University Press, 1984.

James, William. *A Pluralistic Universe: Hibbert Lectures at Manchester College on the Present Situation in Philosophy.* New York: Longmans, Green, 1909.

Kaatz, Martin R. "The Black Swamp: A Study in Historical Geography." *Annals of the Association of American Geographers* 45, no. 1 (1955): 1–35.

Kaufman, Kenn. *A Season on the Wind: Inside the World of Spring Migration*. Boston: Houghton Mifflin Harcourt, 2019.

Kelso, John and James Demers. *Our Living Heritage: The Glory of the Nipigon*. Echo Bay, ON: Mill Creek, 1993.

Kimmerer, Robin Wall. *Braiding Sweetgrass: Indigenous Wisdom, Scientific Knowledge, and the Teachings of Plants*. Minneapolis: Milkweed Editions, 2013.

Köbbing, J. F., N. Thevs, and S. Zerbe. "The Utilisation of Reed (*Phragmites australis*): A Review." *Mires and Peat* 13, no. 1 (2013): 1–14.

Koefoed, Lasse, and Kirsten Simonsen. *Geographies Embodiment Critical Phenomenology and the World of Strangers*. London: Sage, 2020.

Lahood, Adrian. "Scale as Problem, Architecture as Trap." In *Climates: Architecture and the Planetary Imaginary*, edited by James Graham, Caitlin Blanchfield, Alissa Anderson, Jordan H. Carver, and Jacob Moore, 111–118. New York: Columbia Books on Architecture and the City, 2016.

Latour, Bruno. *Down to Earth: Politics in the New Climatic Regime*. Cambridge: Polity Press, 2018.

Latour, Bruno. "Why Has Critique Run out of Steam? from Matters of Fact to Matters of Concern." *Critical Inquiry* 30, no. 2 (2004): 225–248.

Le Guin, Ursula K. *Late in the Day: Poems 2010–2014*. Dexter, MI: PM Press, 2016.

Lefebvre, Henri. *The Production of Space*. Oxford: Blackwell, 1991.

Leski, Kyna. *The Storm of Creativity*. Cambridge, MA: MIT Press, 2015.

Levy, Sharon. "Learning to Love the Great Black Swamp." *Undark* (March 31, 2017). https://undark.org/article/great-black-swamp-ohio-toledo/.

Lewis, C. F. Michael, Steve Blasco, and Pierre Gareau. "Glacial Isostatic Adjustment of the Laurentian Great Lakes Basin." *Géographie physique et Quaternaire* 59, no. 2–3 (2005): 187–210. doi: 10.7202/014754ar.

Library of Congress. "Indian Land Areas Judicially Established." Accessed April 11, 2021, https://www.loc.gov/resource/g3701e.ct008649/?r=0.632,0.222,0.113,0.068,0.

Lipton, Peter. "Inference to the Best Explanation." In *The Companion to the Philosophy of Science*, edited by W. H. Newton Smith, 184–193. Malden, MA: Blackwell, 2000.

Livingstone, David N. *Putting Science in its Place*. Chicago: University of Chicago Press, 2003.

Lockyer, Peter. "Uncertain Harvest: Hard Work, Big Business and Changing Times in Prince Edward County, Ontario." *Material History Review* 33 (1991): 11–23.

Ludwig, David F., Timothy Iannuzzi, and Anthony Esposito. "Phragmites and Environmental Management: A Question of Values." *Estuaries* 26, no. 2 (2003): 624–630.

Luka, Nik. "Contested Periurban Amenity Landscapes: Changing Waterfront 'Countryside Ideals' in Central Canada." *Landscape Research* 42, no. 3 (2017): 256–276.

Lutsky, Karen. "Wild Production: *Phragmites australis* and the Great Lakes Region." In *Productive Landscapes*, edited by Nicolas Koff. New York: Routledge, forthcoming.

211

Lutsky, Karen, and Sean Burkholder. "Curious Methods." *Places Journal* (May 2017). https://doi.org/10.22269/170523.

Lynn-Cooke, Elizabeth. "This Is the Time of Year for Transformation." *Native Sun News Today*, April 3, 2019. https://www.nativesunnews.today/articles/this-is-the-time-of-year-for-transformation/.

M'Closkey, Karen, and Keith VanDerSys. "Down to Earth." *LA+ Interdisciplinary Journal of Landscape Architecture* (Fall 2020): 6–11.

M'Closkey, Karen, and Keith VanDerSys. *Dynamic Patterns: Visualizing Landscapes in a Digital Age.* New York: Routledge, 2017.

Mahood, Kim. *Position Doubtful: Mapping Landscapes and Memories.* Melbourne: Scribe, 2016.

Matson, Laura G.-H., Crystal Ng, Michael Dockry, Madeline Nyblade, Hannah Jo King, Mark Bellcourt, Jeremy Bloomquist, Perry Bunting, Eric Chapman, Diana Dalbotten, Mae A. Davenport et al. "Transforming Research and Relationships through Collaborative Tribal–University Partnerships on Manoomin (Wild Rice)." *Environmental Science and Policy* 115 (2021): 108–115. DOI:10.1016/j.envsci.2020.10.010.

Mattern, Shannon. "Mapping Intelligent Agents." *Places Journal* (September 2017). https://doi.org/10.22269/170926.

McCormack, Derek P. *Refrains for Moving Bodies.* Durham, NC: Duke University Press, 2013.

McGuire, Patricia D. "Wiisaakodewikwe Anishinaabekwe Diabaajimotaw Nipigon Zaaga'igan: Lake Nipigon Ojibway Metis Stories about Women." *Canadian Woman Studies* 26, no. 3/4 (2008): 217–222.

McGuire, Patricia D. "Worldviews in Transition: The Changing Nature of the Lake Nipigon Anishinabek Metis." MA thesis, Lakehead University, 2003.

Meadows, Donella. "Dancing with Systems." Academy for Systems Change. Accessed October 22, 2019. http://donellameadows.org/archives/dancing-with-systems/.

Meadows, Donella. *Thinking in Systems.* White River Junction, VT: Chelsea Green, 2008.

Meier, H., V. P. Perry, and M. A. Davenport. *Perspectives on Climate Preparedness: A Study in the Lower St. Louis River Basin, Minnesota, USA.* St. Paul: Center for Changing Landscapes, University of Minnesota, 2017.

Myers, Natasha. "How to Grow Livable Worlds: Ten Not-So-Easy Steps." In *The World to Come: Art in the Age of the Anthropocene*, edited by Kerry Oliver-Smith, 53–63. Gainesville: University Press of Florida, 2018.

Myers, Natasha. "Ungrid-able Ecologies: Becoming Sensor in a Black Oak Savannah." In *Why Look at Plants? The Botanical Emergence in Contemporary Art*, edited by Giovanni Aloi, 57–60. Leiden: Brill, 2019.

Michigan Department of Environmental Quality. "Salt: A Michigan Resource." Accessed December 1, 2021. http://www.michigan.gov/documents/deq/GIMDL-GGSB_307778_7.pdf.

Michigan State University. "Geography of Michigan and the Great Lakes Region." Accessed December 1, 2021. https://project.geo.msu.edu/geogmich/sugarbeets.html.

212

Midwest Invasive Species Information Network. "Saginaw Bay Watchers." Accessed December 5, 2021. https://www.misin.msu.edu/projects/saginawbaywatchers/.

Milligan, Brett. "Landscape Migration: Environmental Design in the Anthropocene." *Places Journal* (June 2015). https://doi.org/10.22269/150629.

Mitsch, William J. "Solving Lake Erie's Harmful Algal Blooms by Restoring the Great Black Swamp in Ohio." *Ecological Engineering* 108 (2017): 406–413.

Mogen, David. "Re-Evaluating the John W. Campbell Influence: Parochialism, Elitism and Calvinism." *Studies in Popular Culture* 3 (1980): 35–46.

Moore, Gregg E., David Burdick, Christopher Peter, and Donald Keirstead. "Belowground Biomass of *Phragmites australis* in Coastal Marshes." *Northeastern Naturalist* 19, no. 4 (2012): 611–626.

Moore, Kathryn. *Overlooking the Visual*. New York: Routledge, 2010.

Morabito, Valerio. *The City of Imagination*. Novato, CA: ORO Editions, 2020.

Morton, Timothy. *Dark Ecology: For a Logic of Future Coexistence*. New York: Columbia University Press, 2016.

Morton, Timothy. *Humankind: Solidarity with Nonhuman People*. New York: Verso, 2017.

Nelsen, Matthew P., Robert Lücking, Kevin C. Boyce, Thorsten H. Lumbsch, and Richard H. Ree. "The Macroevolutionary Dynamics of Symbiotic and Phenotypic Diversification in Lichens." *Proceedings of the National Academy of Sciences* 117, no. 35 (2020): 21495–21503. https://doi.org/10.1073/pnas.2001913117.

Nelsen, Matthew P., Robert Lücking, Kevin C. Boyce, Thorsten H. Lumbsch, and Richard H. Ree. "No Support for the Emergence of Lichens prior to the Evolution of Vascular Plants." *Geobiology* 18, no. 1 (January 2020): 3–13.

Norton, Richard, Lorelle Meadows, and Guy Meadows. "Drawing Lines in Law Books and on Sandy Beaches: Marking Ordinary High Water on Michigan's Great Lakes Shorelines under the Public Trust Doctrine." *Coastal Management* 39, no. 2 (2011): 133–157.

Ontario Geological Survey. "Record MD152A16NE00004." Ontario Mineral Inventory. Accessed February 2, 2021. http://www.geologyontario.mndm.gov.on.ca/mndmfiles/mdi/data/records/MDI52A16NE00004.html.

Ontario Power Generation. "Northwestern Ontario Communities." Accessed February 5, 2021. https://www.opg.com/building-strong-and-safe-communities/our-communities/northwestern-ontario/.

Oreskes, Naomi. *Why Trust Science?* Princeton, NJ: Princeton University Press, 2019.

Palmer, Laurie. "The Lichen Museum." In *Why Look at Plants? The Botanical Emergence in Contemporary Art*, edited by Giovanni Aloi, 149–154. Leiden: Brill, 2019.

Panci, H., M. Montano, A. Shultz, T. Barnick, and K. Stone. *Climate Change Vulnerability Assessment: Integrating Scientific and Traditional Ecological Knowledge*. Great Lakes Indian Fish and Wildlife Commission, 2018.

Pandey, Vimal Chandra, and Deblina Maiti. "Phragmites Species—Promising Perennial Grasses for Phytoremediation and Biofuel Production." In *Phytoremediation Potential of Perennial Grasses*, edited by Vimal Chandra Pandey and D. P. Singh, 97–114. Amsterdam: Elsevier, 2020.

213

Pevzner, Nicholas, and Sanjukta Sen, "Preparing Ground." *Places Journal* (June 2010). https://doi.org/10.22269/100629.

Phillips, Rasheedah. "Dismantling the Master's Clockwork Universe." *In Space-Time Collapse 1: From the Congo to the Carolinas*, edited by Rasheedah Phillips and Dominique Matti, 15–31. Monee, IL: House of Future Sciences, 2016.

Pierre-Louis, Kendra. "Want to Escape Global Warming? These Cities Promise Cool Relief." *New York Times*, April 15, 2019. https://www.nytimes.com/2019/04/15/climate/climate-migration-duluth.html.

Port of Green Bay. "Cat Island Chain Background and Access Guide." Brown County Port and Resource Recovery Department, 2018. https://www.portofgreenbay.com/cat-island-restoration-project/.

Pradhananga, Amit, Mae Davenport, and Emily Green, "Cultural Narratives on Constraints to Community Engagement in Urban Water Restoration." *Journal of Contemporary Water Research & Education* 166, no.1 (2019): 79–94. https://doi-org.proxy.library.upenn.edu/10.1111/j.1936-704X.2019.03303.x.

Pradhananga, Amit, Emily Green, Jennifer Shepard, and Mae Davenport. "The Influence of Community Attachment and Environmental Concern on Climate-Related Civic Engagement in Lake Superior's North Shore Region." *Journal of Coastal Conservation* 25, no. 26 (2021). https://doi.org/10.1007/s11852-021-00816-5.

Reo, Nicholas, and J. Ogden. "Anishnaabe Aki: An Indigenous Perspective on the Global Threat of Invasive Species." *Sustainability Science* 13, no. 5 (2018): 1443–1452.

Rice, Brian. "Bridging Academia and Indigenous Environmental Science: Is It Too Late?" In *The Nature of Empires and the Empires of Nature*, edited by Karl S. Hele, 67–84. Waterloo, ON: Wilfrid Laurier University Press, 2013.

Rifkin, Mark. *Beyond Settler Time: Temporal Sovereignty and Indigenous Self-Determination*. Durham, NC: Duke University Press, 2017.

Royal Botanic Garden Edinburgh. "Lichens in the City: Short Film." March 2017. YouTube Video, 10:42. https://youtu.be/oyaB18pL_3c.

Ryle, Gilbert. "The Thinking of Thoughts: What Is 'Le Penseur" Doing?" In *Collected Essays 1929–1968: Collected Papers Volume 2*, edited by Julia Tanney, 494–510. New York: Routledge, 2009.

Samuelson, P. A. "Reaffirming the Existence of 'Reasonable' Bergson–Samuelson Social Welfare Functions." *Economica* 44, no. 173 (February 1977): 81–88. https://doi.org/10.2307/2553553.

Sandwell, B. K. "Us Amphibious Canadians." In *Pocketful of Canada*, edited by J. D. Robins. Toronto: Collins, 1946.

Scott, Nancy. *Lake Nipigon: Where the Great Lakes Begin.* Toronto: Dundurn, 2015.

Serres, Michel. *The Natural Contract.* Ann Arbor: University of Michigan Press, 1995.

Serres, Michel, and Bruno Latour. *Conversations on Science, Culture and Time.* Ann Arbor: University of Michigan Press, 1995.

Simon, Herbert A. "Designing Organization for an Information Rich World." In *Computers, Communications and the Public Interest*, edited by Martin Greenberger, 40–41. Baltimore: Johns Hopkins University Press, 1971.

Skrepichuk, Peter, and William Skrepichuk. "Vert Island Sandstone: A History in Images Part 1: 1880–1895." *Papers and Records*, Thunder Bay Historical Museum Society, 2016. https://www.thunderbaymuseum.com/wp-content/uploads/2017/12/PR-2016-low-res.pdf.

Slemp, C., M. A. Davenport, E. Seekamp, J. M. Brehm, J. E. Schoonover, and K. W. Williard. "Growing Too Fast: Local Stakeholders Speak Out about Growth and Its Consequences for Community Well-being in the Urban–Rural Interface." *Landscape and Urban Planning* 106, no. 2 (2012): 139–148.

Snook, Debbie. "Ohio's Trail of Tears." Wyandotte Nation. Accessed November 26, 2021. https://wyandotte-nation.org/culture/history/published/trail-of-tears/.

Solnit, Rebecca. *A Field Guide to Getting Lost.* New York: Viking, 2005.

Srivastava, Jatin, Swinder J. S. Kalra, and Ram Naraian. "Environmental Perspectives of *Phragmites australis* (Cav.) Trin. Ex. Steudel." *Applied Water Science* 4, no. 3 (2014): 193–202. DOI: 10.1007/s13201-013-0142-x.

State University of New York School of Environmental Science and Forestry. "Indigenous Science Letter." Accessed September 15, 2019. https://www.esf.edu/indigenous-science-letter/Indigenous_Science_Declaration.pdf.

Stettler, Reinhard F. *Cottonwood and the River of Time: On Trees, Evolution, and Society.* Seattle: University of Washington Press, 2009.

Stren, Olivia. "Prince Edward County: O Canada! Tastefully Riding the Food Trends, This Slice of Ontario Knows How to Please." *National Geographic Traveler* 24, no. 7 (2007): 121–122.

Stults, M., S. Petersen, J. Bell, W. Baule, E. Nasser, E. Gibbons, and M. Fougerat. "Climate Change Vulnerability Assessment and Adaptation Plan: 1854 Ceded Territory including the Bois Forte, Fond du Lac, and Grand Portage Reservations." Duluth, MN: 1854 Ceded Territory, 2016. http://www.1854treatyauthority.org/environment/climate-change.html.

Sundberg, Juanita. "Decolonizing Posthumanist Geographies." *Cultural Geographies* 21, no. 1 (2014): 33–47. DOI: 10.1177/1474474013486067.

Temple, Stanley A. "The Nasty Necessity: Eradicating Exotics." *Conservation Biology* 4, no. 2 (1990): 113–115.

Thün, Geoffrey, Kathy Velikov, Dan McTavish, and Colin Ripley. *Infra Eco Logi Urbanism: A Project for the Great Lakes Megaregion.* Zurich: Park Books, 2015.

Tiffin, Edward. "Collections and Researches." *Pioneer Society of Michigan.* Lansing: Wynkoop Hallenbeck Crawford, 1880.

Tiles, J.E. "Experiment as Intervention." *British Journal for the Philosophy of Science* 44, no. 3 (1993): 463–475.

Todd, Zoe. "Indigenizing the Anthropocene." In *Art in the Anthropocene: Encounters among Aesthetics, Politics, Environments, and Epistemologies*, edited by Heather Davis and Etienne Turpin, 241–254. London: Open Humanities Press, 2015.

Tribal Adaptation Menu Team. *Dibaginjigaadeg Anishinaabe Ezhitwaad: A Tribal Climate Adaptation Menu.* Great Lakes Indian Fish and Wildlife Commission, Odanah, WI, 2019.

Tsing, Anna Lowenhaupt. *The Mushroom at the End of the World*. Princeton, NJ: Princeton University Press, 2015.

Turnbull, David. "Maps, Narratives and Trails: Performativity, Hodology and Distributed Knowledges in Complex Adaptive Systems." *Geographical Research* 45, no. 4 (2007): 140–149.

United Nations. "Convention on the Law of the Sea." Article 10. Accessed September 4, 2019. https://www.un.org/Depts/los/convention_agreements/texts/unclos/unclos_e.pdf.

United States Army Corps of Engineers U.S. Waterways Experiment Station. *Experiments to Determine the Backwater Effects of Submerged Sills in the St. Clair River*. Vicksburg, MS: War Department USACE, Paper 16 (April 1934). https://apps.dtic.mil/sti/pdfs/ADA622857.pdf.

United States Environmental Protection Agency. "Physical Features of the Great Lakes." Accessed December 2, 2021. https://www.epa.gov/greatlakes/physical-features-great-lakes.

Walton, Jessie. "Forgotten History of Ohio's Indigenous Tribes." *Midstory* (July 2020). https://www.midstory.org/the-forgotten-history-of-ohios-indigenous-peoples/.

Waters, Thomas F. *The Superior North Shore*. Minneapolis: University of Minnesota Press, 1987.

Way, Thaïsa. "Landscapes of Industrial Excess: A Thick Sections Approach to Gas Works Park." *Journal of Landscape Architecture* (Spring 2013): 28–39.

Weitzman School of Design. "From the Rooftops: Anu Mathur." July 6, 2020. Video Lecture, 27:42. https://vimeo.com/435738233.

Wilson, C. F. Walking Dredge. US Patent 1,289,589, filed April 10, 1916, and issued December 31, 1918.

Wolff, Jane. *Delta Primer: A Field Guide to the California Delta*. San Francisco: William Stout, 2003.

Wright, J. O. "Swamp and Overflowed Lands in the United States: Ownership and Reclamation." United States Department of Agriculture. Washington, DC: Government Printing Office, 1907.

Yong, Ed. "The Overlooked Organisms That Keep Challenging Our Assumptions about Life." *Atlantic*, January 17, 2019. https://www.theatlantic.com/science/archive/2019/01/how-lichens-explain-and-re-explain-world/580681/.

Yoon, Carol Kaseuk. "Decade-Long Question Results in Rich Paean to Lichens." *New York Times*, January 1, 2002.

Zolli, Andrew, and Ann Marie Healy. *Resilience: Why Things Bounce Back*. New York: Simon and Schuster, 2013.

Zumthor, Peter. *Thinking Architecture*. Basel: Birkhäuser, 2006.

INDEX

Note: References in *italics* refer to figures.

218